Abuse + Alcoholism, equals Murder?

Larry I Patterson

～ Written from true events ～

Abuse + Alcoholism, equals Murder?
Written from true events
Copyright © 2019 by Larry I Patterson

Library of Congress Control Number: 2019914102
ISBN-13:   Paperback: 978-1-950073-73-3
*   ePub: 978-1-950073-74-0*

All rights reserved. No part of this publication may be reproduced, distributed, or transmitted in any form or by any means, including photocopying, recording, or other electronic or mechanical methods, without the prior written permission of the publisher or author, except in the case of brief quotations embodied in critical reviews and certain other noncommercial uses permitted by copyright law.

Although every precaution has been taken to verify the accuracy of the information contained herein, the author and publisher assume no responsibility for any errors or omissions. No liability is assumed for damages that may result from the use of information contained within.

Printed in the United States of America

GoToPublish LLC
1-888-337-1724
www.gotopublish.com
info@gotopublish.com

CHAPTER ONE

~≫ Part one ≪~

It is around seven in the evening, a policeman is just escorting Eva to the police car. Karla drives up, and after parking her car, she gets out, and as she is running up to Eva and the policeman she raises her arm, and waves her hand as she says, "Oh- Oh— hello there please, excuse me officer, but I am her daughter-in-law! As she catches up with them, she takes a couple of deep breaths, and she says, "Can you please tell me where you are taking her?"

"Hello ma-am," the officer replies, "I am taking her to the Johnson County Jail in Cleburne for questioning."

When the police and Eva get to the Jail, The police officer put her in a room with a table, and a few chairs, and a large mirror, but nothing else, as one of the police officers stay with her. A little later a couple of detectives come into the room to talk to her.

One of the detectives sits down across from her and says, "Hello Eva, I am detective Jeff Moran, I am investigating the death of your husband, and you know that he passed away, right?"

"Yes I know he died," Eva wipes her eyes with a tissue, then says, "I didn't want him to die, and I did not shoot him!"

The Detective gives her another tissue, then says, "We are going to ask you to tell us in your own words what happened. We are going to tape, and record this conversation, and I would like you to start from the beginning."

She is still all freaked out, but stuttering and sobbing she tells them, "It all started when my husband got home around six o:clock pm, I had been sleeping all day, and he went into work for me at the storage place. He must have been drinking alcohol before he left the storage place, because when he got home he woke me up, and he started bad mouthing me. He hit me in the head, for not going to work today, all because he had to take my place. I had gotten tired of him bad mouthing me, and I went to my room, and looked in my mirror to see what he did to my face, and to nurse where he hit me. I was looking in the mirror and I seen this object under the pillow, and went there, and found it was a gun, I picked it up, and I went into the room where he was, and I found him already lying on the floor."

After finishing the interrogation the officer writes out a confession, she says, "I do not have my glasses." But she tried to read it anyway, and signs it.

She has been there at the jail and in the same room for about five hours. She talked to the detectives earlier, and now it is after midnight, and she finally did eat something (after reaching the hangover stage), and she was able to keep the food in her stomach. Her head starts to clear, and she is feeling much better. Being all alone in this small room she becomes bored, and starts reminiscing back to events that happened earlier this morning.

As I woke up in my own bed, I am feeling like I can't even move one finger, much less my whole body. I knew very well why I felt so lousy, and my mind and body felt like lead, and not a hangover. My body is never depleted of alcohol long enough to go into a hangover state. I am at the end of my rope, physically, and mentally. I can see no reason for me to get up to go to work, to eat, or even to go on living. Boy! I sure let myself go to pot, I have always managed to pull myself out of these funks when I go this far, and I get disgusted with myself, and my actions.

This time I knew I was not going to pull myself out. I had gone too far, and slid down into my sink hole, and I cannot climb back out, and I can't find any reason to try anymore, I can't even find God anymore. But I dragged myself up out of bed, I really don't feel up to getting dressed and going into work. I braced myself against the wall, as I stumbled the short distance between the two rooms. I knowingly know what Mr. M's reaction is going to be, when I ask him to go to work in my place for me. I just knew he would call me all sorts of lazy good for nothings. I am hoping that he won't call me any bad names as he usually does, especially in front of our grandson.

I had began drinking when I started dating Mr. M, before that I just drank when partying. Mr. M always seemed to have a drink in his hand, and it never seemed to affect him. Not so with me, but I tried to keep up with him. Early on when our kids were small we only had a couple of drinks at night at home.

But we always drank when we went out. But as time went on, and our problems got bigger and bigger, our drinking grew in proportion. Mine especially, since I started using it as a crutch to cope with my marriage, of which had gotten abusive, and a life style that I didn't like much anymore.

I found out that as long as I didn't have a thought of my own, or an opinion of my own, or make waves of any sort, life with Mr. M was great. But it seems that I am, or just a little, or maybe a whole lot, spoiled. I have a temper, and I am stubborn as a mule. As I matured it didn't take long for me to get pregnant.

"She gets pregnant every time Mr. M hangs his pants on the bed post." my mother used to say. Although I was only pregnant five times, twice by my first husband, which one was miscarried, and the rest with Mr. M, of which one was also miscarried, this was before I turned twenty six. After my last miscarriage I pleaded and begged and talked myself blue in the face trying to convince my dear husband not to have any more children, but we had one more.

Now we have living at home with us my daughter from my first marriage, and my oldest son Gordon and by this time I was already tired of being the responsible one. I was the one stuck at home being the good little wife, and mother, going to PTA, being room mother, and all of that. While Mr. M went on with his care free life, with no changes, I didn't like that for a hoot, especially when I didn't want any kids in the first place.

My job is being the manager of two self- storage units. As I walked into the kitchen where my husband Mr. M, (Everyone calls him that, but I call him Mat.) and our grandson Michael, were eating breakfast. "Mat, you might not like this, but I am feeling sick, and I really can't go into work today, would you mind going in for me?"

"Well I am thinking, I do have something else I wanted to do today," says Mat "but I guess I'll have to go in for you, since you can't get off your lazy butt and go in and do your job like your supposed to, you could go to work if you stayed off of the booze. But, are you hungry? and if you are, I wouldn't mind fixing you something to eat? It may make you feel better, and I like to feed people."

"Well I really don't feel like eating anything because my stomach is so queasy." All of a sudden I make a dash into the bathroom and throw up.

As I come out of the bathroom I hear Mr. M mumbling, "She is a sorry sot all of her drinking is the reason she cannot go into work, or do anything else." he says this as he is stomping around the kitchen fixing Michael something to eat.

"Grandma, I am sorry to hear that you are sick."

"Thank you so much Michael, I am sorry that I could not be around you more this weekend, but I haven't been feeling very well."

"That's okay Grandma, me and Grandpa had fun together this weekend."

"Mat, I am going back to bed." Not wanting to hear anymore of his abuse, I leave the kitchen, and go back to the bedroom, then lay down on the bed. He wasn't to bad this time, as he usually follows me back to the bedroom, harassing me and calling me bad names.

Then I hear him say to Michael, "C'mon boy let's get you to school."

"Okay Grandpa, I am ready, and thank you for taking me to school."

"Not a problem Mickey, you are not a problem to me at all, I wish I could say the same thing about your grandma."

When I heard that I sighed a big relieve, and relaxed, and went to sleep. I remember waking up around three o:clock pm, My head is spinning, and my stomach feels like somebody just punched me there, and being an alcoholic I felt like I really needed a drink, Mr. M keeps all the liquor and/or booze locked up in the safe, and I don't know the combination, and the bottle that I had hidden in my closet is empty, and I am not in any shape to go to the store.

I get up, and finding nobody home I call Mr. M, and as he answers the phone I say, "Mat, can you come home, I really do need a drink?"

"Okay Eva, I will pick up Michael from school, and will be home as soon as I can."

"Oh thank you Mathew." I hang up, and go back to bed. Suddenly I come back to reality when a policewoman opens the door, and comes into the room, and says to me, "Come with me please." She takes my arm, and escorts me to another room, and she tells me, "Take off all your clothes, and put them in this bag," as she hands me the bag. Then she says, "There is a shower in there, take a shower! then put on these clothes that are on that bench." She points to a phone on the wall, and says to me, "Call me on this phone when you are finished." Then she leaves the room, and she closes the door. I get undressed, and put all my clothes into the bag, and then take a shower. After I get dressed I call her on the phone. Then she comes back in, and says, "Follow me." She escorts me to a cell (of which I will be in all by myself) which has a big window, and as I enter she closes the door. Later on I notice a man outside watching & talking to me. Apparently they put me on a suicide watch.

Part Two

It is around seven o:clock in the evening a policeman is escorting Eva to the police car. Karla drives up, and after parking her car she gets out, and as she is running up to Eva and the policeman, she raises her arm, and waves her hand as she is saying, "Oh-Oh—hello there please, excuse me officer, as she catches up with them she takes a couple of deep breaths, and she says, "I am her daughter in law, can you tell me where are you taking her?"

"Hello ma-am," the officer replies, "I am taking her to the Johnson County Jail in Cleburne, for questioning."

As she walks toward the house, another officer says, "I cannot let you come any further towards the house, as this in now a crime scene."

Karla asks the police officer standing there, "Can you tell me what happened?"

"This is an ongoing investigation, and I am not allowed to say anything, the crime scene investigators have closed off the premises, you will have to back up."

As she is backing up, she is thinking, "I still have a lot of questions," but her thoughts are interrupted when the two paramedics come out of the house with an empty gurney. "What is happening? Where is Mr. Mathews? Is he alright?"

As the paramedics get closer to her one of them says, "The police are waiting for the Medical Examiner to get here, he will take the body to the morgue."

"Body!—-you mean Mr. Mathews.

"I am so sorry, but Yes."

Karla starts to cry, and says, "Are you telling me he is dead?"

"Yes, I am sorry for your loss, but he has bled out, we tried our best, but to no avail, even if we had gotten here sooner, I don't think it would have made any difference, as I think he was dead shortly after he hit the floor."

She's in tears; she turns around and sees the police car leaving, and see's Eva looking out the window, and crying and waving. Sadly and still crying herself Karla waves back at the police car, and thinking to herself, "She really looks bad." Then she says out loud, "I don't think she could have done it, is there any way that I can go with her?"

The officer says, "No not at this time, maybe you can go later, but the detectives want to talk to her first.

As Karla gets into her car. She takes in a deep breath, and lets it out slowly. She calms down, although she is still crying, as she is looking in her glove compartment for some tissues, and finding some she clears her nose, and wipes her eyes, and then she starts her car, and drives home. She arrives at her apartment house, and walks to her neighbor Sally's apartment, where she left her son.

She knocks on Sally's door, and she is still crying while waiting at the door, and she starts wiping her eyes and nose with another tissue. When the door opens, Sally is standing there as Karla says, "Thank you so much for watching Michael for me especially, with such short notice, I really do appreciate it."

"I know things happen—-I'm glad I was able to help." as Sally closes the door behind her, she is saying, "What happened over there? If you don't mind me asking."

"The police wouldn't tell me anything, but I will keep you in the loop."

Just then Michael and his friend Jeffery come running up to his mom, and says, "Hi Mom, gees that didn't take very long, but why are you crying?"

"I will tell you tomorrow, but right now we are going home, and at nine o:clock sharp you are going to bed."

When they get home, and at nine o:clock she says "Goodnight Michael," as she put her son to bed, then goes into the kitchen and she takes out a bottle of wine that was left over from the weekend, and pours some into a glass, and sitting down, she takes a couple of sips of the wine, after a few more sips she starts calming down. She says to herself out loud, "Oh I miss my husband so much, and I could really use him now." Then she starts reminiscing about things that happened earlier, leading to the final happenings of that day.

I am remembering that it was on Monday afternoon on January 10th 1994, here I am living in this little town of Burleson Texas, which is just outside of Fort Worth. I had a party on Sunday evening, and Monday morning I got up early, and I went to work, and after working all day I was glad to get home as I arrived at my door. After opening it, I walk into my apartment and look around, as I am standing there I see the mess, the beer cans, glasses, and bottles, all over the apartment, it really did look like I had a party here. As I am thinking, "It didn't look so bad when I left this morning."

I remember saying out loud, "Oh I really do need to clean this up before I bring my son home." My son is seven years old, and is staying at his deceased Father Parent's house over the weekend, as he really enjoys being with them."

I had given a party at my apartment over this last weekend; because over the New Year's holiday the both of us had flown to Fremont California to visit my Mom & Dad, and the rest of my family, and all of my close friends. I had moved to Burleson about two years ago, a year after my husband Martin died.

I go into my bedroom, to change, from my work clothes, and get into something more comfortable, something that I can work at home in. Just as I start to pick up the mess, I tell myself out loud, "I know one thing for sure I will not have another party here—for a long-

long time!" Just then the doorbell rings, and as I open the door I see standing there two good friends of mine, Joan, and Mary; who both go to the same college as I do; and they were both at the party.

"Oh! What a surprise Come on in." I remember saying.

"Hi Karla," Mary says, "we stopped by to help you clean up, because we knew what kind of mess that was left after the party, and we knew you would be getting home about now."

"We would have helped you clean up last night," adds Joan, "but it was getting late, and I guess we might have had a little bit too much to drink, and we know that you had to get up early to go to work."

"I understand," I remember saying, "I really want to thank you both, as I can surely use the extra help."

I get out the vacuum cleaner, and start vacuuming. Joan and Mary start picking up the beer cans, bottles, etc., and putting it all in some garbage bags. With the three of us working together, it didn't take too long to finish, I went into the kitchen, and made a pot of coffee, and offered them some sweet rolls that were left over from my breakfast. The three of us sit down at the table, and start reminiscing over the happenings of the party. After the coffee break, and after getting all the bags together, we each take one; and together we go down the stairs to the garbage bin. After putting the bags into the garbage bin; we all walk to where their cars are parked.

I give Mary a hug, and she says to me, "Goodbye Karla, and thanks for inviting me to the party, I will see you later."

I answer back, "Thank you so much for coming over here, and helping me, and thanks for coming to the party, I will see you later."

Then I turn to Joan and give her a hug, "Goodbye Karla," she starts to walk towards her car, then she turns toward me, and says, "I also want to thank you for inviting me to the party, and I will probably see you later in our English class."

"Goodbye Joan', I said, and I really do want to thank you for coming over here, and giving me a helping hand to clean up, and I will see you later"

Both of the women get into their own car, and leave. As they leave, I return to my apartment, I climb up the stairs, and as I enter the apartment, I remember giving a big sigh, "Oh-my, what a difference", as I am thinking to myself, "After all of that work, I can use a drink." Then I go into the kitchen, and take out a bottle of wine.

I sit down to relax, and pour some wine into a glass, I slowly take a sip. As I relax, I start thinking of the time I met my husband Martin I still after three years miss him very much; mostly because right now I am not seeing anyone; and I am getting ready for another semester at the college. I stop thinking about what happened today, and I start thinking back to the year of 1983.

I was going on eighteen, and just graduated from high school in Fremont, California, I am remembering the day like it was just yesterday. It was on June 19th, my sister Marlene's 20th birthday. Some friends of mine invited Marlene and I to a surprise party they were giving for her. On the day of the party, our next door neighbor who was going to the beauty college to be a hair stylist, came to our house, and washed Marlene's and my hair, then she put my blond hair up into a really nice and fancy pony tail, and Marlene's auburn hair she curled and blown dried it. After putting on some makeup, Marlene's husband Kent, and the two of us left for the party in Marlene's new car.

After we arrive at the party, we all start to go inside, and everyone inside was waiting by the front door, as Marlene went in, they all yelled out "SURPRISE!!" to her. I know Marlene was not expecting that. Later I was walking around in the house meeting some of the other people that I didn't know. (I guess in my own flamboyant way, I don't know many strangers). I look up and see this tall handsome guy, around six feet seven inches tall or so, walking towards me. As he gets close to me, I see that he is smiling on one side of his mouth, and he says with a great Texas accent, "Hi! My name is Martin! And what may I ask is your name?"

As I am smiling back I simply say, "My name is Karla Henderson."

Martin replies, "I know we are at a party, and you look like you are not with anyone, but Karla, how would you like it if I get you some punch?"

I answer, "Yes, I am not with anyone other than my sister Marlene, and yes I would like some punch. Thank you."

Martin finds a chair, and I sit down. Martin leaves, and he walks to where the drinks and goodies are. He soon returns with a couple of glasses of punch in one hand, and a plate of goodies in the other.

He says, "Here is the drink I promised you, take your pick," as he offers a pink lemonade, and a strawberry punch in his right hand, as he says, "I didn't know which one you would like, so I took one of each," then he says to me "Here are some goodies that were offered."

"Oh thank you so much," I said, "I will take the pink one."

I keep thinking, as I take the glass, and notice how large his hand is, and I am thinking to myself, "no wonder he can carry two glasses so easily in one hand." Later after we drank our drinks, and ate the goodies, the music starts, and everyone starts dancing.

We start dancing together, I remember how awkward I felt, as I was not wearing high heels and he was so much taller than me, but he was such a good dancer, we danced quite a few more dances together. When the party was over, Martin says to me, "Can I offer you a ride home?"

"I am only seventeen, and my parents are very strict that I get home with my sister. That is my sister over there," as I am pointing at Marlene, "You know the birthday girl, but thank you for offering."

"Maybe I can get your phone number, so I can call you later?" Martin replies, "I really would like to get to know you better, I know now that you are seventeen, but maybe we can go out on a date with your parents' consent?"

I say to him smiling, "I guess so— Sure, I will give you my phone number, but remember I still live at home, and I will think about the date." I get a piece of paper, and a pen, and write down the number, and I hand it to him.

Later after Marlene takes me home, I remember her asking, "Who was that tall guy you were dancing with?"

"His name is Martin, and he is from Texas. He us a friend of Carl Kinsley, you know the guy that was going with your friend Debby. Then

I said, "I think I like Martin I gave him my phone number, and what do you! think? —-maybe, I could go out with him?"

I remember Marlene saying, "Oh yeah you know what, I do remember Carl Kinsley, and yes I think it would be okay if you went on a date with Martin, but it should be a double date with me and Kent, at least, on your first date."

Well we did, and we went steady for about a year or so. In October 1984, Martin was in the Navy, and stationed on the same Air Craft Carrier based in Alameda California, that Carl Kinsley was stationed on. Martin told me the ship was leaving port, and was being re-stationed to the East Coast near Norfolk Virginia. Martin did not want to take the cruise, so he took a leave, and decided to ride his motorcycle to his new port. I remind myself as I am thinking, "He asked me to go with him, and I really did want to go, but it would be against my parents' wishes."

So Martin went by himself, and a few months later, he was on leave again, and he came back to Fremont in a blue Toyota Sports Car that he had left at his Parents' house in Texas before he went into the Navy. As he was coming here, He stopped at his parent's house, picked up the car, and drove it here, (leaving his motorcycle there at his parent's house). After a few dates, he asked me to marry him. We got married, and left for the east coast together in the Toyota; I didn't worry about a place to live when we got there, as Martin had already gotten a furnished apartment before he left, now that I think about it, I guess he was pretty sure of himself.

In February 1987 Martin got out of the navy, and we drove together in the Toyota to Burleson Texas, where we stopped to see his Mom and Dad. After we arrive, and after all the hugs, and kisses, Martin says to his Mom, "Mom this is Karla."

"So this is Karla" his Mother says to Martin, and looking towards me she says, "I am so glad to finally meet you, Hmm, and you are quite pretty, and I guess I am not surprised to see that you are pregnant, when are you due?"

"I am so glad to meet you to Eva, and thank you for the compliment". I answer then I say, "The baby is due in July."

"Mom we are going to stay here for a few days," Martin says, "then we shall go on to California'"

After those few days were over, we left for California, Martin rode the motorcycle, and I drove the Toyota sports car."

All of a sudden I was startled by someone ringing the doorbell, and I just realized where I am, as I go to the door, I open it, as I am looking around I find that no one is there, but seeing a package on the step, I assumed the UPS man, or the Mail Man left it there. I take the package, and confirm that it was from UPS. I open the package, and inside is a skirt and blouse that I ordered from a mail order catalog. As I turn toward the kitchen I look at the kitchen clock, and I say to myself, "Oh-Oh it's time to go pick up my son Mickey at his grandparents' house."

I put things away, then I leave my apartment, and get into my white Malibu Chevy, and as I start to drive to my in-laws house, I back up from my parking spot, and start to pull out into the driveway this car all of a sudden speeds up behind me, swerves to the left of me, then passing me, and cutting in front of me, and making me come to a complete stop. Then he turns right onto Stuart Blvd. After he makes the right turn, he speeds towards the stop sign, (about three hundred feet) and not even slowing down, he turns left on Burleson Blvd. in front of some moving vehicles, causing them to stop suddenly, and that causes an accident. I still am thinking, "What an idiot that guy is, I hope he doesn't live around here." But I get through the traffic and all without too much trouble, and continue on.

As I arrive at my in-laws house, I knock on the door. The door opens, and my son Michael says, "Hey mom, I am glad you are here, I am ready to go home." as he gives me a big hug, and a kiss.

I enter into the house, and ask my son, "Where is Grandma?"

"She is in the bedroom I guess," Michael answers. Then he says, "Grandma has been in bed all day as usual, she is not fun anymore, all she want's to do is sleep. "After she got up this morning, she told Grandpa that she wasn't going to work. I don't know, but maybe she might not have been thinking to well or not feeling too well, as she went back to bed she went into the wrong bedroom"

"Oh!" I said, "Well, okay I guess that makes sense, but where is grandpa?"

"He picked me up at school," Michael answers, "And was going back to work."

"Okay, I am going to wake Grandma up now, and let her know that I am taking you home, you can stay out here, and watch television until we are ready to leave." As I enter into the bedroom, Eva opens her eyes, and sees me standing there, as she is not quite awake yet, she is slurring her words, as she says to me, "Oh! Karla,—I guess you are taking Michael home now?"

"Yes," I answer. Then I say, "You are not looking very good, are you sick?"

She says without slurring her words, "I just didn't feel like going in today."

"Is there something I can get for you?" I ask.

"No," Eva says, "I am fine I will just sleep it off."

"So what did Michael do all weekend?" I ask.

"I don't know," Eva says, "He was with his Grandpa most of the time."

"Before we leave, Can I get you something?"

"No thanks," Eva answers I am fine for now thank you."

As we are leaving I turn off the television; I go to the back door, and I make sure it is locked. Then I walk to the front door; with Michael in front of me, I lock and close the front door; then Michael and I get into my car, and drive off. When we get close to home, and I see this same car that passed me sooner, in the gas station. I say to Mickey, "When I was coming over here to pick you up, that car over there in the gas station is the one that passed me, and caused an accident, and that is him standing over there in the blue coat, do you know him?"

"I don't know him, but I see him around the apartments a lot, hanging around with Joe, he's the guy standing next to him, Joe lives somewhere in the apartments."—-Karla stops reminiscing, and then she goes to bed. The next morning Karla gets up, gets Michael off to school, then gets into her car and drives to Cleburne Johnson County

Jail. She walks in and says to the sergeant behind the desk, "I am here to see my Mother-in -law that was brought in last night around seven o:clock."

He says, "What's her name?"

"Her name is Eva Marie Mathews."

Okay, here it is," the officer says, "She is still here, but visiting hours are at 10:00am."

Can you put me on her list so I can get in to see her?" Karla asks. "Sure," he says, "What is your name, and what are you to her?"

Karla looks up at him funny and says, "My name is Karla Henderson, and I am her daughter-in-law. And I will be back at 10:00am. And what is her bail?"

"I don't know as yet, when you come back she should be out of court by then."

"Fine," she says. As she leaves the police station, and heads into work.

CHAPTER TWO

Back at the Mathews, and after Karla and Michael left, Eva is lying there trying to go to sleep, but starts thinking back in her life, and to what a total waste everything had turned out to be. I remember my mother telling me, "Eva you was born in a storm cellar in Waurika, Oklahoma, in the year of 1936 during a tornado." I was raised there until I got married to my first husband, and we moved to South Carolina, although I am thinking, I have been in some kind of a storm all of my life. I was the thirteenth child born of my mother, although there were only eight of us kids living at home. I guess I grew up with some violence, as I always said; "I was born standing up and fighting, back; as we were always brawling over something."

Until I was three or four, I was very angry, resentful, and mean; now that is not normal for a kid that age. I'm quite sure I wasn't born that way, so how did I get so nasty so quick? It might have been the fact that I was the youngest, and all the other kids would pick on me, and I resented it, and fought back. I was told that I was a nasty, mean, spoiled brat, but I don't remember any of that.

But it seems I was a hell raiser, chasing my Niece (although she still loves me.) with bricks, threatening to brain her, pouring buttermilk over my sister's head (she was four years older than me), and hitting my uncle in the head with a stick of stove wood. I don't recall being punished for any of these things, which was strange because my Mother was a very strict mama. My goodness, she had to be with raising that many brats.

Later on I asked my older sister, "How come my Mama never punished me for all the things that I did that was wrong?"

My sister told me, "Mama always said, 'Because you were the baby in the family." This seemed strange as my Mama was part Indian. She was around one sixteenth part Indian blood from being able to draw royalties, or whatever Indians get from the government. My Mother was all of four feet eleven inches tall, she was pretty much a runt next to my father.

I remember one incident when my little mama had had enough of my long tall Texas grown daddy's drinking, and nonsense. He had gone to town, and spent all of his wages drinking, (or whatever he did there). I heard tales that he cut a mean swath in the bars there, (Mama had gone in there and dragged him out of a few). That day he had done his thing in town, and finally came home drunk with hardly enough food to feed us. As he sat leaning back on two legs of his chair at the table, and spouting off in a drunken drawl, my little Mama came around the table, and kicked his chair out from under him. He landed flat on his back in total surprise, and she landed on top of him with a big butcher knife at his throat. Then proceeded to tell him what was what, and how things were going to go from then on. I don't remember his words, as I think all of us kids were sitting there in total shock. But I do recall that my Daddy never touched another drop of alcohol from that day on.

I remember another incident when my oldest Sister Edith, was still living at home with us. Edith and I were going to take a trip to Mexico, but to get in and out of Mexico I needed a birth certificate. My sister and I went to the court house where they keep all the records.

I asked the man in charge, "Can you give me a copy of my birth certificate."

He said, "Fill out this form, then I will find it for you." The form asks: What is your name, and when were you born and what is your mother's name?

"Give me the form." I write: My name is Eva Marie Worthington, and I was born on May 24, 1936, and my mother's name is Martha Worthington.

He had a hard time finding any record of my birth certificate, and he said, "There is no name of Eva Worthington anywhere listed I need someone to verify the date you were born."

As my sister was with me she told him, "Yes I verify that she was born on that date."

The clerk found my certificate under my mother's name. The hospital registered the certificate before I was named, (actually I found out later that I wasn't named until three weeks, after my birth) the clerk made out the certificate, but he misspelled my name as Evan. (Is that adding insult to injury or what?) I said to him, "My name is not Evan, and please change it to Eva right now.

The clerk says, "I am sorry Eva, it was my mistake, I will change it right now, I wouldn't want you to go the rest of your life as Evan, now would I?"

I answered him, "No certainly not!"

When I was a teenager, my youngest brother Tommy dragged me around everywhere he went. I remember he would take me hunting, fishing, and we would go into some road houses, dives, or whatever he was doing. He was following the rodeo circuit, and he would ride broncos, and bull's. When he was close to home I went with him to the rodeos, and some of the other rodeo rider's would ask me to ride their horses, and exercise their horses for them. I really did like to ride the horses, and I always wished I had one of my own, but that didn't happen. I really think my brother would have liked a younger brother, instead of a sister as we used to fight, and wrestle like two boys; maybe that is why I grew up as a tom-boy, I had no use for any girly things at all, until I was old enough to discover boys, and make the transition from tom-boy to girly-girl with no problem.

We had a great time together until this one time when we were in a road house, I stepped between him and another guy he was about to fight for no reason, and as he swung his fist; he hit me instead, and knocked me down. Then he was running around like an idiot yelling, "Who hit her, I'll kill the Sob."

I told him, " **You**! Hit me,"

Talk about getting red faced, he spent a whole week trying to make it up to me, by taking me places like Wichita Falls to visit my sister, and buying me things. It was fun while it lasted which to my mind was not long enough.

But I was determined to complete high school, and I finally did, as I was the only one in the family that did graduate. After high school I tried to join the Air-Force, and I passed all the tests. Then I chickened out, and met this real great guy who was always responsible, and considerate of me, and my feelings most of the time, and he was in the Air Force, and was in the Air force Police, stationed at Sheppard air force base in Wichita Falls, Texas. We got married, and had a child, and He was later transferred to Greenville South Carolina, where we moved.

After four years of marriage in the year 1959, my husband was to be deployed to Japan. Our daughter Sherrie was three year old, and I am really looking forward to going with him." I really wanted to go as I like to do new things, and I knew I would never get the opportunity do go again. I couldn't believe he didn't know me well enough to know I would probably thrive over there.

My husband says, "I don't think the two of you will be okay over there, and I have decided not to take you with me."

I believe he was listening to other people, and not to me I was shocked, and I was looking forward to going, and I say very angrily, "If you don't take me with you, don't expect for me to wait for you to come back."

I think I knew then that our marriage was over, because actually we were too young, no matter how well we got along, and we did great for how much we cared for each other. But no matter what I said changed his mind, I did wonder about that, because he was not that selfish, and normally would have wanted us with him, and that turned me against him even more.

"Fine," he says.

We left our trailer in South Carolina, and he left Sherry and myself at my parents house back in Oklahoma, where we decided we would stay while he was in Japan, I was not happy! My parents lived miles out in the country in a very small frame house, (a glorified shack) the same place where I grew up. It was four small rooms with no bath room, no plumbing. The only modern convenience was the electricity. This was not so bad, but bad enough, I had enough of this when I was growing up. The only good thing was that there was no other kids living there.

Looking back to when I reached my teens, and I wanted to have friends come in to visit, this never happened. My friends would come and pick me up, and I would stay with them at their house. My parents never had any type of vehicle ever. I was blessed that my friends didn't seem bothered that I was dirt poor, and wore hand me down clothes, or whatever my mother made for me from scrapes. I look back now and wonder how I ever had the guts, and stimulus to make it through high school with hardly any money, or clothes, or any thing else.

I was blessed that other people liked me, and seemed to want me around, so I had a lot of friends, and was welcomed into their homes. Quite a transition from the spoiled brat of my early years, to the well behaved, well mannered, teenager I grew into.

But I regress getting back to Robert leaving me to go overseas to Japan without me. Leaving me, to hold down the fort; as we had a new mobile home on a rented lot, a fairly new car that had mortgages to be made back in South Carolina. Very shortly the country life got the best of me, and I packed mine, and Sherri's possessions into the car, and headed to Wichita falls where my sister lived.

Bearing in mind that I had just learned to drive before Robert left, as I surely would need to be able to drive, stuck out a hundred or so miles in nowhere land. I did have a little practice driving my Mom around on errands occasionally, but not much, and mostly on country dirt roads with not much traffic. But brave me I take off like a veteran driver, in my Chevy to Wichita Falls , and the wide open spaces.

Naturally living with my sister didn't work out well either, as I am a woman now with a child of my own, and I am used to living in my own home. So I decided I wanted to be back in that home, despite the fact that we had rented it out to some friends while Robert would be overseas. Once more I packed up my little Chevy, and headed to Greenville South Carolina where we were living before Robert was deployed. The trip was essentially uneventful except when I was driving about ninety miles an hour, and going over some railroad tracks, and hit the air. It didn't scare me at all. I decided I liked driving , as I was in control, and I like driving fast for whatever reason I don't know, unless I like taking chances.

Not a thought to Sherries safety. See what a responsible person I am. Bless her, she would stand in the seat next to me, (before seat belts, and car seats etc.) and yell "Get out of my mama's way."

Cute huh? And she was my cutey with blonde curls, and big blue eyes, which later turned brown. She was tiny, and I dressed her in ruffles from head to toe most of the time. Boy did she enjoy being cute, and a girl. She caught on quick, and used it to her advantage.

The only other thing that happened on this trip, was in Alabama. I was stopped at a traffic light waiting for it to turn green, when a car hit me in the rear end of my car. I hardly felt it, but the guy got out, and so did I. After talking awhile, the decided he would ride along with me in my car, and his buddy could follow in his car. I don't remember why I decided this was okay, I don't know what he looked like his name or anything else, even where I left him, or he left me. But apparently he was good company for awhile.

I finally got to Hartwell Georgia, this is where my husband's family lived. We stayed there while the people in my trailer were finding a place to live, and later they moved out. We finally got moved into my trailer, and was content, until reality hit me. I had bills, and not enough money coming in to stretch. I only had a corporal's allotment, which is not a whole lot. When Robert was home we had his pay, plus my allotment to live on. Now that he was gone I didn't have that. I guess I wasn't thinking about that when I decided to move back home or I was probably thinking as the young do, that I would manage some way.

Turned out that was a lot harder than I thought. I applied for jobs everywhere I could, while my next door neighbor watched Sherrie for me. No one would hire me, I had no experience or whatever. Finally I was desperate, and my daughter and I were eating a hot dog a day, so I took a job running a rural paper route. It was good because I could take Sherrie with me, and I didn't have the child care worry. Again I don't recall details but I do remember winning all the contests, and doing okay, and my boss was nice. The probable reason for this is because I could dress as I pleased and I pleased to wear short shorts and tank tops like Daisy Mae in Dukes of Hazard. I also met my second husband at this time.

The place that I picked up my papers to be delivered, was at his place of business. When I first met him, I was scared cross eyed, because when he came in he would growl at me. I would pick up my papers, and run away, this went on for quite a while. He was a large built person around six feet tall, and had huge shoulders, and large all over, but had a wonderful personality.

But one night I was feeling kind of lonely, but adventurous, and ready to take a chance, so I drove to his place. He was there in his office playing cards with some of the friends from Donaldson Air Force Base, where Robert had been based until he went overseas. I asked one of the guys who worked for Mr. M, to take a message to him for me. The message said, "If you can tear yourself away from the game, we can go out, and you can buy me a drink." He was out of his office in record time.

As it turned out I didn't wait very long after that, and I divorced Robert, and I fell in love with Mr. M, although he is twelve years older than me. He was born in Georgia, but reared in South Carolina, and he has a very charismatic personality. He is a salesman, and I always thought that he has the ability, and the know how to do anything, and if he couldn't he would have it done. At twenty-two I thought myself as challenged, as he was married, and I being threatened by his wife, and several other of her women friends, all of them much older than me, as I feel I am out of their league.

Although at the time I am basking in the attention, and having a good ole time, and I really did enjoy being the other woman. I was more than ready to have someone take over, and take care of me and my daughter at this point in time. Mr. M is excellent at taking over, and before I knew it he had taken over my life.

Mr. M owns a car dealership, and gas station, but is primarily a car salesman at the dealership located on a major highway in Guerneville, SC. He has plenty of money, and doesn't mind spending it. He has a lot of friends wherever he goes. We go out together day or night, and he will introduce me to any of them with no regards of hiding our relationship. I didn't want a hidden relationship either, and I am pleased he takes me everywhere. We go out together a lot, we would go to Georgia, or Florida, as we both love to dance, and we are pretty good together, as we complement each other.

I fell head over heels in love with him. He loved me, but not like I loved him, he was first in my life along with my daughter. Mr. M had been married eleven years, and never had any children, but Sherrie and I come along. What I couldn't figure out after his eleven years of marriage to his first wife, is that everything that he put his wife thru, she still fought for him tooth and nail, even as she knew about me, and some of the other women in his life. I guess that shows what kind of man he is. I worshiped him, and the ground that he walked on. I was obsessed with pleasing him, and trying to make him love me as much in return.

I didn't really want any more kids when I had Sherrie, it actually scared me cross eyed. I was responsible for her, she wasn't a doll like I day-dream about, she is a living breathing human being that I am responsible for, and heck, I can hardly take care of her. But bless her heart, she is thrown here, and there, while I am going out with Mr. M, but she is never neglected, and she is always loved.

After all that thinking Eva falls asleep, and an hour or so later she wakes up, then she gets up, and walks slowly to the bathroom, and relieves herself, then goes back to bed. Again she lies down and tries to sleep but starts thinking back again and mulling over her messed up life.

This one big mistake I made, moving to Burleson Texas, it turned out to be the biggest mistake of my life. I think Mr. M had joined the 'KKK', and turned into a Red-Neck Levis, and Boot wearing foul mouth cussing, gun toting ill-mannered idiot. He is no longer the suit wearing, tie bearing person he was. Mr. M is a big man and he like to intimidate, and use physical force to impress, or scare people. Funny thing is, most of the time I was not afraid of him. I do not like him anymore, but I still love him, even after all the bullying, abusing, and trying to control me.

After looking back, I can see the imperfections as well as the perfections. But well into our marriage, and all the heartaches, life stayed good for us at times. With Mr. M there was no security, no responsibility, we would be rolling in luxury one day, and near starving the next. I decided to get my own car, credit cards, etc. as my credit was perfect but his credit stunk.

One time before we were married, but living in Fort Worth, I started driving back to South Carolina, when my car broke down just a few miles outside of Dallas Texas. I had the car towed to the nearest dealership, and called Mr. M whom was in South Carolina already. I stayed at the dealership of course, as Mr. M flew in to Dallas, but he could not get there until later. The manager of the dealership offered to take me out to dinner, and then on to the airport to meet Mr. M.

The manager took the both of us to a hotel, and we got a room. Mr. M didn't like it for the manager to take me out to dinner, and he was furious with me, but he never said anything to the manager. Mr. M and I argued, and Mr. M had gotten really physical with me, and he starts to choke me, and threatens to throw me out of the seventh floor hotel window. He cooled down, and didn't do it, but that time I was a little shook up, to say the least.

Later after we married, I went to work as a respiratory therapist technician, and helped save a lot of lives then, as there are a lot of stories there, but I am not going to think about that right now. After nine years, I loved being a respiratory therapist technician, but doing the same thing all the time, I got bored, and I decided to go to college. After taking so many classes, I had to select a major. Of course everything I have taken was to further my medical career. I found out it was impossible to move up in the respiratory therapy, so I applied for the regular nursing program. This program was extremely hard to get into as there was so many trying to get in, but they took me in on my first try. For the next five years I worked full time, and went to school full time, maybe getting four hours sleep every day.

After graduating nursing school, and passing the medical boards, I worked five years in the ICU unit areas of the largest hospital in Fort

Worth, the Harris Methodist Hospital. Five years is much too long to work in any ICU, two years is plenty of time to get a burn out, and get high blood pressure, and stress yourself out. I knew that sometime in the future I was going to leave Mr. M, and I wanted to be totally independent, if I wasn't already.

This one incident stands out in my mind, one night I got home late from work, around eight pm., I had gone out with some of the friends that I work with for drinks, and something to eat. When I did get home Mr. M and my two boys, Gordon, and Martin were in the kitchen. Gordon is fifteen, and standing by the refrigerator, and Martin is thirteen, and about six foot two inches tall, and is sitting at the table. I come in, and Mr. M jumped up, and grabbed me by my shirt, and jacket, and tore them down to my waist. Then he hit me knocking me down, and kicking me with his steel toed boots. I had no idea what was happening, or why it happened in the first place.

My youngest son Martin jumped up and yelled! "Don't you hit my momma again?"

Mr. M got the strangest look on his face, like someone had thrown ice water on it. Or maybe it was that he couldn't believe someone had the nerve to tell him to do something, or that someone would actually take up for me, especially one of his sons. Then Mr. M just turned around and walked out the door. That episode was the end of Martin, and his dad's relationship. It wasn't any good to start with, as Martin didn't like or approve of the way of his dad.

Martin said to me, "I don't like him or anything he did, early on."

After that as Martin got older and grew to six ft. seven inches, he said to his dad, "I don't have time to play your silly games."

I often wondered how Martin was able to just ignore his dad, when Gordon and I were jumping through loops, trying to please him, which we never did. Things just went from bad to worse after that. Our marriage and home became a battle ground with the kids fighting right along with us. We were divided, with my daughter, and Martin on my side, and Gordon with his father on the other side. Sherrie my daughter from early on, would get into our fights, and usually get hit as well. She was the one who normally called the police."

All of this would happen after I gave up, or gave in, and I would take him back. After the first time I left him (Which was at best ten years into the marriage?) I am not one to just jump into things, and I made him promise several things before I would take him back. Number one is to go to marriage counseling. I think he went one or two times. It was all off when he was told he might have some problems. He refused to believe he had any faults, that I was the one who had problems, so I needed to fix me.

He was a champ at putting me and Gordon down, and nothing we did was worthwhile, and he loved to bait me in front of others, until I lose my temper, and make a fool of myself. Then he would sit back, and say, 'Look what I have to tolerate.' He had everyone fooled into thinking he was perfect. He treated us like we were made of glass. He never let his guard down in public, and everybody liked him. He was very charismatic, and just plain charming, especially with women. They all adored him, and he was a wonderful dancer, which they seemed to love, and so did I. He was a heck of a guy, except I couldn't live with him. So we rocked along for several years, because I didn't want to leave him, or my home, etc…

As I am going through these burn outs, and overly stress, it is during this time my daughter had a baby boy, and she disappears leaving him with me, as she hasn't been heard of since. After a few years, and a lot court dates, I took custody of my grandson Billy, and having two sons of my own, I start to drink pretty heavily. I finally leave Mr. M, and I move to Arlington Texas (which is about half way between Dallas, and Fort Worth).

My oldest son Gordon had taken a trip to California, and was involved in an accident with his motorcycle, and almost killed him. I made the trip by myself with an itinerary that Mr. M had written for me (Like I was too stupid to function on my own).

After I got back to Texas, I had moved back in with Mr. M for a while, but things got worse, so I gave up, and decided to leave again, and lined up a job in Houston Texas, I thought it might work out better for all if I put some miles between us. I resigned my job with the promise to the hospital that if the job didn't work out in Houston, that I could return to my job here.

I told Mr. M, "Mat I am going to California with my sister to visit her daughter in Los Angeles."

Mr. M answers, "When are you leaving?" "We are leaving this weekend." I say to him.

The day before I was leaving with my sister, I got me, and the car ready to go to town, and I drive to my friend's house, as they were having a going away party for me, they were giving me six hundred dollars that they collected for me. What a group of good friends, to do that for me. My friend has an unlisted phone number, but while I was there my husband called, and I could tell he was quite angry, and he had been drinking heavily. I knew he must have found out from some way that I was leaving him, and going to Houston when I come back from Los Angeles. It was probably from my sons, as I wanted them to go with me, but they refused, because they wanted to stay there with their friends.

My husband could find out anything, just like an unlisted phone number. I was really uneasy, but I had to go home, although I sure didn't want to, just because of the way he talked to me on the phone, and it scared me. Nothing was mentioned about me leaving. Yep I have to admit that time I was really scared, I went home, and went in, as nobody was home, which made me more uneasy. I didn't have any idea where the boys were. I called my sister on the phone, and told her what time I would pick her up the next day. As I hung up the phone I heard a banging on the front door, I didn't know who it was, as Mr. M, and the boys have their own keys.

I opened the door, and Mr. M came in, and he hit me in the face with his fist, and knocked me down, and I slid all the way down the hallway, and over the couch.

I pulled myself together, and getting up I said, "Mat what did you do that for?"

Then he hit me again. After that I decided that things were getting very serious. I was thinking that I should be quiet, and stay out of site. I went into our bedroom, which is on the other side of the den, and the boy's bedroom. He went into the kitchen, and made himself a drink, and followed me into the bedroom. We started to argue; when he threw the drink, and the glass he had, into my face. I put my hand to my face, and found blood on my hand, and ran down my arm, I didn't know how bad I was hurt. Now I am really scared. I didn't know what he was going to do. But I was thinking that I was not going to get out of there alive.

He left, and went back to the kitchen to get himself another drink. I sneaked by him, and went into the boy's room; I knew Gordon had a gun in there on a gun rack that he had made. I reached for one, and opened a drawer, and pulled out a shell, and loaded it into the shotgun, not knowing if it was the right one or not, but it did fit. I walked back into the den, and he came in, as he came towards me he was cussing, and he started to raise his arm, and I pulled the trigger, and prayed. The gun fired, and the bullet hit him in the groin causing him to lose his testicles. I call that divine intervention.

I called the police, but they never came out, they told me to come to the station when I could, and make out a statement. I guess they knew about the abuse. They did send an ambulance for Mr. M. The police deputy did come the next day, to take some pictures of my injuries.

I went to California with my sister, and then went on to Houston from California. I was totally worthless in Houston eaten up with guilt, and missing the boys, so I came back with my tail between my legs.

My son Gordon told me, "I would have rather that you stayed away if it would keep the peace."

That really hurt me, but I understand his point of view. At some point Mr. M became a totally different man during, and immediately after recovering from the injuries that I bestowed upon him. Unfortunately it didn't last, and soon things were pretty much the same except for the physical abuse. He didn't hit me anymore, but poured the mental and emotional abuse to full blast, and nobody was any better at it than he was.

The doctor and my friends believe he was punishing me because of his injuries. I found out later that they replaced everything, and even enhanced what he had left. He refused to take the hormone shots like he was supposed to. I kept hoping that he would mellow out with old age, but he got more hateful and nasty. He even started the physical abuse again. So now we are back to square one.

My youngest son Martin left home, and joined the navy, and after serving four (4) years on active duty he settled in California marrying a young lady Karla, and together they had my second grandson Mike, but we call him 'Mickey'.

My son Martin was living across the bay from San Francisco, and was on his way home from work, on the day after Halloween in 1987, and he was killed in an accident while riding home on his motorcycle. I went to California again on my own, because Mr. M missed three flights, but he finally shows up with his sister holding his hand.

When I got there, we went to the hospital where Martin was, Karla, and her Mother were there. Afterwards I met up with the doctor, he told me, "The blow that he received in the accident has caused his brain to swell, we drilled a hole in the back of his head to relief the pressure, but his brain had swollen too much, and he didn't make it." The doctor then said, "Things might have been better for him if he had been wearing a helmet."

But Karla told me, "Martin was always stubborn, and always said," "If I have to go, then I will go without a helmet,"

Karla continues, "and he always refused to wear it."

Mr. M and his sister start a wrongful death civil suit, as the man that hit the motorcycle that Martin was riding on, ran a stoplight, and the court ruled in Martin's favor, and awarded my grandson an award that he would get when he turns eighteen. Mr. M then left me to take care of everything else, as I take Mike's body back to bury him in Texas, although all of his friends had a nice service for him before we left, even though Martin wasn't there.

This time when we returned to Texas, I was in bad shape with the drinking, and the loss of my daughter, and my son Martin. I don't give up easily, but I had given up. I was hospitalized with dehydration, and malnutrition in critical care. I never slept except when I knocked myself out with booze, I was physically and mentally addicted. The doctor's said I could not get off the alcohol addiction without help, and it would eventually kill me. So my husband locked up all the liquor in a safe, and took parts out of my car so I could not go to the liquor store, and he would hide my wallet. I worked as a nurse, and the last few years I worked, was in an intensive care unit at the hospital. I retired from nursing in 1991, because my alcohol problem was getting too much to be safe anymore.

As I remember Mr. M thought, "I am helping her by locking up the liquor in a safe, and keeping all of the money out of her reach, and taking parts out of her car, but making sure she gets to the AAA meetings in time twice a week."

But I say, "Locking up the bottles of liquor anywhere in the house, is mean and cruel, because an alcoholic will go crazy knowing the liquor is close by."

CHAPTER THREE

After all that thinking Karla finally falls asleep. While Mr. M is still at work he has a few drinks. He leaves work, and when he gets home around six o'clock he goes into her bedroom, and wakes her up, and he is feeling the drinks he had earlier, and says to her in an loud tone, "Thanks a lot for not going to work today."

She says, "Please forgive me honey; I am sorry I wasn't feeling well enough to work today, and I am still not feeling well."

He goes into the kitchen and opens a can of soup, and pours it in a pan, then he put the pan on the stove to heat it up, and as he is looking at her he says, "If you eat this I will make you a drink." (All the time he is warming up the soup he is badmouthing her, and calling her names.)

"Okay, I will try and eat it," After she eats the soup he fixes her a drink; he is still calling her names as he hands it to her. He goes into the den and makes himself a drink, and as he is making his drink he continues calling her names. Later as she walks into the room where he is, she walks right up near to him, but not looking directly at him. As she turns toward him she sees him swinging his right arm, as he slaps her real hard on the left side of her head.

She quickly put her hand to her head, and starts rubbing it where he hit her, she says, "What did you do that for?"

"The house is all a mess, you haven't done anything all day." Then he sits down in his easy reclining chair in the living room, with his back to the bedroom.

Eva is tired of hearing the entire badmouthing and bad name calling, and she is upset at him for hitting her, and is trying to get away from him. She goes into the bathroom, and throws up what she just ate, she thinks she heard some loud noise, but she then swallows down the drink, and says to herself, "I am surprised I didn't spill any." After being in the bathroom for a while, she leaves and then quickly turns around, and goes back into the bathroom, and throws up the liquor she had just drank.

After she leaves the bathroom she walks past the room he is in, and she slips by it. She passes by quickly, and as she went by she thought she noticed someone else in the room, but continues into her bedroom, and closes the door. As she walks closer to the bed, she notices something under the pillow, she goes over and picks up the pillow, and sees a hand gun lying where the pillow had been on the bed, and she doesn't remember ever seeing the gun there before, but identifies the gun as a .38 caliber hand gun that Mr. M always kept in the glove compartment of his pickup, of which he never locks. Anyone that knew him would have access to the gun in his truck. She doesn't know how it got under the pillow.

She walks over to the bed and picks up the gun, when she enters into the room where he is, she is prepared to show him the gun, but as she looks down she is startled by seeing Mr. M lying on the floor on his back, bleeding from his stomach. She places the gun on a counter. All of a sudden she starts freaking out when she sees all of the blood on the floor, and suddenly she becomes aware of what is happening. She panics, then she picks up the telephone, and nervously her hand is shaking, she can hardly hold onto the phone, as she pushes the fast dial number to Karla's phone.

Karla answers, "Hello."

Eva is very nervous, and stuttering says, "Karla! Mr. M has just been shot! and he is not moving! What am I going to do?"

Karla says, "Please slow down Eva, I can hardly understand you, I think you said that He is not moving, but— is He breathing?"

Eva is so nervous, and shaking, she says in a stuttering voice, "I don't think so; can you come over right away?"

Karla answers, "Yes I will be right over, after you hang up, call 9-1-1. okay?"

Eva answers, "Okay, but get over here as quickly as you can." Eva hangs up the phone, then dials 9-1-1. "Hello this is 9-1-1 what is your emergency?"

Eva says in a very nervous, and stuttering voice, "Hello, My husband has been shot and is bleeding, and I don't want him to die."

The operator says, "I know you are nervous, but calm down, I can hardly understand what you are saying—I need to know what your address is?"

Eva tells her the address.

The Operator says, "Okay, I want you to calm down, help is coming to you right away? Are you okay otherwise?"

Eva answers, "Yes I guess so."

The operator says, "Is there anyone there with you?"

Eva says, "No, there is no one else here."

Eva hangs up the phone then she sits down next to him, she is holding him in her hands. It seems like forever before two officers of the Burleson police department arrive.

The officer yells out, "Hello! Police! Open the door!" as they find the door locked.

One of the officers says, "Let's go around to the back door."

The other officer says, "Okay you go, I will stay here just in case someone tries to leave." The officer continues around to the back door, and finding the back door also locked. The two officers at the same time force open both doors. As they enter into the house they meet up with each other, and they both hear a women crying, and they continue to walk to where she is. As they enter into the room they find the woman on top of the man lying on the floor. The emergency team arrives about that time, and enters thru the front door. The paramedics proceed to the room where the rest of them are, and finding the woman still on top of Mr. M, they pull her off of him, as she is fighting them, crying, and literally freaking out.

As the two paramedics pull Eva off of Mr. M, another police officer from Johnson County enters into the room, he goes to Eva, and gently, but firmly escorts her to the side of the room, and says to her, "What is your name?"

"My name is Eva, and my husband lying there on the floor is Martin." The officer says to her, "Hmm what happened here?"

Eva answers with a stuttering voice, "I don't know, I walked into the room, and found him lying there on the floor, bleeding."

"Is that gun there on the counter the one that was used?" Asks the policeman.

"I don't know, I found that gun under a pillow in the spare room where I have been sleeping all day, and set it there when I found him, I don't know how it got under that pillow, maybe I should have left it there. Then she says, "All I am wearing is a white robe, do you think I can go to my bedroom, and put on some clothes?"

"Sure, this is your room here?" answers the officer.

"No, this is the spare bedroom," she answers.

"If all you are wearing is that robe, then I will wait here until you put some clothes on, and then we will go to the police station, where a detective will ask you some more questions."

Eva looks at him, and smiles, then goes into her bedroom, and put on some clothes.

Part three

It is around seven o'clock in the evening, a policeman is escorting Eva to the police car. Karla drives up, and after parking her car, she gets out, and is running up to Eva and the policeman, she raises her arm, and waves her hand as she says, "Oh— Oh. Hello there, excuse me officer, when she catches up to them, she takes a couple of deep breaths, and says, "I am her daughter-in-law! Can you please tell me where you are taking her?"

"Hello ma-am," the officer replies, "I am taking her to Johnson County Jail in Cleburne for questioning."

That night because she is an alcoholic, and freaking out, the officers put her on a suicide watch. The next morning they escort her to the court room where she was appointed a public defender, and charged with murder, the judge set bail at one hundred thousand dollars.

After leaving the court, he escorts her to a phone so she can call someone to post bail for her. She dials the phone for her son Gordon, and he answers and says, "Hello."

"Hello Gordon this is your mother, I am at the County Jail and I need you to come and bail me out."

"Sorry mom but I cannot do it," as he hang up his phone, she angrily hangs up also.

She says to the officer with her, "He hung up on me, and I can't understand why he won't put up the bail, the property is worth more than enough."

Eva is sitting in a cell later on, and she is thinking back, "The detectives wrote out my confession, and I signed it, although I was in total shock, and I could not read it because I didn't have my glasses on, and a matter of fact I never did get my glasses. I was on a complete quilt trip, and I was ready to hold out my arm for the needle.

I was a total basket case (as they refer to me at the jail), and I went into the DTS plus throwing up all over the place, as I was coming off the alcohol. But would you believe that they were all extra nice to me, all of the officers, the sergeant, and the lieutenant had me brought to his office, they had me in irons, and the whole works. The first thing the lieutenant did was to take off the restraints, and he threw them against the wall, and that was the last I seen of them.

The Lieutenant asked me questions about Mr. M's activities, nothing to do with why I was there. I stayed in a private cell for about a week, until I settled down. The lieutenant had ordered me some Valium, and a liquid diet. After the week they put me into the main holding cell with all the other women prisoners. Going in I was scared silly, and I almost climbed up the side of the lady officer's frame, that was escorting me. I have never been in that situation before, but the officer talked me down, and promised I would be alright, and all. She was real sweet.

Because the jail in Houston was full, and overcrowded, they moved a lot of the women prisoners from Houston into the jail at Dallas. These gals were tough, and I didn't have enough sense to be scared of them, or maybe it was because I was still on the Valium, which is almost solid alcohol. After a couple of months everything seemed to settle down a bit as Eddie was not scared of anything anymore.

CHAPTER FOUR

Eva stayed in the jail in Johnson county until late June almost five months, until the trial was about to begin. When going to the court house she was allowed to wear civilian clothes (which Karla had brought to the jail), and they allowed her to change into them before being transported to the court house.

Karla had given up her apartment, and moved into the Mathews home, and is paying the mortgage for Eva. On Saturday the 25th she went to the jail house, and left some clothes that Eva could wear to the court house, and she visited with her for a short time.

On Monday June 27, 1994 Karla got up early to call Micheal's school; after she dials, someone answers and says, "This is the Hamilton Grade School, Marie speaking, how can I help you?"

"Hello, this is Karla Henderson, and my son Michael Henderson goes to this school. I am going to take him out of school this week."

"Hello Karla, may I ask why you are taking Michael out of school for a whole week?"

"Yes of course," Karla then says, "I am taking him out because his grandmother is on trial for murder, and I want him to be there. Also I would like him to make up his school work somehow."

"Okay Karla I will tell his teacher, and she can get back to you later."

"Fine, and thank you for everything." Karla hangs up, and reminds herself, "I don't have to worry about me, as I am now on vacation."

After they eat breakfast, Michael and Karla get into the car, and drive to Cleburne for the trial. They get to the court room, and Karla sees Eva's friend Eudora, and her daughter Carrie standing there ready to go into the court room. She walks up to them and says, "Hi Eudora, and Carrie how are you?"

Eudora is smiling as she answers, "Oh! Hello Karla! I am just fine, and I am so glad that you are here—how about the four of us sit next to each other in the court room?"

"Yes Eudora! I would like that." As they come into the court room, they see Eva already sitting at the defendants table. The four of them take a seat in the back row. Eva turns around and waves at them, but she cannot talk to anyone. Eudora, and Karla, Carrie, and Michael all get settled down. As Karla turns around and sees behind her, Eva's family is entering into the court room, as they all walk past Karla and Eudora.

Edith the sister of Eva's is the first one and says "Hi Karla, and Eudora."

Jean also a sister of Eva's walks by accompanied by her husband Bill, and says, "Hello Karla, Eudora, Carrie, and Hi Michael."

Then they were followed by Tommy a brother to Eva, as he walks by he says, "Hello Karla, Eudora, Carrie, and Hello there Michael."

The four of them all say in unison, "Hello."

They were followed by the rest of the family. Continuing on they sit in the first row behind the bar. Then Karla turns around and sees Mathew's family come into the court room and no one says anything, and they all sit on the opposite side of the center aisle. Then Karla Eudora, Carrie, and Michael all get up, and sit in a row right behind Eva's family.

A few minutes later, the Judge comes in, and everyone in the court room stands up. The bailiff says, "This 249th District Court, in the city of Cleburne, of Johnson County in the state of Texas, with Judge Wayne Bridewell presiding, is now is session."

"Good morning everyone, and thank you, and you all can be seated. The next case is the case number 027951002 of Eva June Henderson, with the felony charge of first degree murder of Edwin Irvine Henderson." After he said that, he read thirteen pages of the charges, after he finished with that he then says, "Will the defendant please rise, and as they rise he says, "How does the defendant plead?"

Eva looks like a woman that would be in the jury selection, and what they would look like; her grayish hair is brushed back from her face; and she is wearing a very attractive blue pant suit; she looks kind of nervous; but occasionally smiles at her defense attorneys: Shelly Fowler, and Sybil Stuebing. Eva and her two lawyers are standing together, as Eva answers, "Not guilty your honor."

Judge Bridewell says, "You all can sit down, and Bailiff you can now call down to the jury room, and have them bring in the prospective jurors now." After a few minutes around sixty prospective jurors enter into the court room quietly, and sit down as the Judge says, "Voir dire questioning of prospective jurors will begin next, and will continue after an early lunch recess this afternoon." Then Judge Bridewell says, "I hopefully expect a jury to be chosen by quitting time today. Testimony in the case will probably start when court convenes at 9:00am tomorrow if there is a jury selected."

Then Judge Bidwell also states, "This morning, the defense filed a motion for a continuation in this case due to 'Pre-trial' publicity of an article printed in the Times-Review paper over the week-end. I am denying the motion, but will allow attorneys from both sides to bring up the subject of publicity during questioning of the jurors. The Judge looks out at the prospective jurors, and says, "The trial will probably last a week."

Around three o'clock the jury was finally selected on that day June 27th, 1994 consisting of nine men, and three women. The Judge states to the court, "The trial will convene on Tuesday June 28, 1994 at Nine am."

Later in her cell at the Jail, Eva starts thinking again, "It is great to wear decent clothes again, as I lost some of the weight I had gained from all the drinking. When leaving for the court house his morning I felt pretty confident, and I was all prayed up, so I was just waiting to see what would happen. It was well known about Mat's and my situation, I really feel that if the Burleson police were in charge things might have gone differently.

We had moved about five miles from Burleson, which put us in Johnson County, where Mr. M and I built our home. Because of us moving there, I belief the sheriff and his posse took over. I believe the Sheriff and Mr. M were 'Friends' as were the District Attorney. While I was at home I heard their names quite often, and I knew they talked a lot via the phone, and etc.

As my family came into the court room, and everyone in the court room was standing, a warm feeling came over me as I looked around and seen most of my family standing there, and I smiled, but they couldn't speak to me, or me them. My sister Edith from South Carolina became emotional and broke down, bless her heart. She spent most of the time of the trial in tears. To my family they were in shock as I had kept most of the abuse, and my situation hidden, like most abused wife's do.

There were a few people though, that spent a lot of time visiting in our house, and knew about the abuse. My husband would gradually let his guard down if people were around long enough. Of course I wasn't allowed to touch anyone or they me, and for some silly reason, I have always put up a front, and tried not to upset anyone.

My older sister Jean, (whom is deceased now) and her husband Bill, (whom is also deceased) both came from South Carolina, along with my brother Tommy, from Oklahoma, and all of them were there for the duration of the trial. My sister Edith testified for me, along with my friend Eudora, and her daughter Carrie. My Brother Tommy got upset with my lawyer at one time, and he said, "I want you to fire her, and get someone else."

I said to him, "I won't let you. One attorney as far as I am concerned is as good as another. I had experience with them when I was going for the custody of my grandson Billy, I don't trust them at all, and I don't want you to waste your money."

The District Attorney offered me a plea bargain of twenty years; I didn't understand why they (the detective, district attorney, another attorney, and my attorney) were pressuring me to accept the bargain. My attorney admits that she didn't want to try this case in this court, as they were known to give big sentences, and no time served. They probably would have dropped the time frame, if I would have bargained for it.

I have always backed up when someone was trying to pressure me into anything, so I refused to bargain, or even consider a plea bargain. That was my biggest mistake; I might have saved myself and my family all that money. During the trial, for some reason, I don't know why, my lawyer would not let Karla testify for me, as she was there with Mickey the whole time. The only thing the district attorney had against me was that I was an alcoholic, and I didn't get any help, but that was a lie.

For some reason they couldn't get my treatment records from any place or any of the records from the police in Burleson, where we had lived before we bought four acres, and built the house in Johnson County. The witnesses against me all lied, including the sheriff's deputies. I believe that they are allowed to do that without any reprisal.

I am thinking, "I believe my grandson Billy's testimony, and Ruthie's was the ones that convicted me. Billy is my daughter's son; I took custody of, and raised. I believe that the District Attorney bribed Billy by taking care of some parking and traffic tickets for him He was eighteen at the time, and had abandonment issues, as he saw this as me leaving him, I am sure. He said, "I didn't see any abuse in twelve years I lived there."

Ruthie was a girl that worked for us, and we treated like a daughter. She was crazy in love with my son Eddy, he was angry at me so that made her angry at me also, they were kids, and didn't realize the intent of what they were doing. Ruthie said, "I didn't see any abuse."

A neighbor that lived about a quarter of a mile across the street from us, is a black man, and he is married to a white lady, he also said, "I didn't see any abuse." He and Mr. M were both from Georgia, and South Carolina, and hit it off. He was at our house quite a bit, and he was there one night when I had to call the police on Mr. M. Another time I climbed out the window partially naked, and went to their house running from Mr. M, the black guy thought I was crazy.

This all happened after I started drinking heavily; otherwise I probably wouldn't have panicked like that. But when he testified he said nothing about any of that.

The officer that escorted me at the trial got angry at Billy for testifying against me, and checked his record with the police. He didn't have anything on record otherwise the officer would have arrested him right then.

My friends and family were furious when they heard that the family on Mr. M's side was talking with everybody, including the jurors, and the witnesses. My attorney was told, and she said, "Nothing has changed."

The trial started on the Monday before the Fourth of July holiday, and the judge told everyone the trial should be over by the end of the week. What an idiot I am. Or maybe it was all those years in a relationship where I felt I couldn't ask, or dare to ask, or made to feel I didn't deserve to be given, or treated with kindness.

I remember my attorney some time during the trial asking me, "You are not used to anyone being nice, or kind to you, are you?"

I answered, "My marriage was just an extension of my childhood. I grew up with nobody really caring about my welfare, or so it seemed. I didn't complain or ask for anything, not even attention, because it didn't do any good. I was pretty much ignored, or so it seemed. So I withdrew with a big giant chip on my shoulder, leave me alone, or suffer the consequences, I had a temper, and struck out without thinking or caring. Of course over all the years I have learned to control this by the time I married Mr. M or, I would have had to learn quickly. But I still had a lot of back bone, and pride, and fought back a lot."

CHAPTER FIVE

On Tuesday morning Judge Bridewell calls the court to order at exactly 9:00a.m., and then asks the prosecution attorney, "You can now start your opening statement."

The District Attorney Assistant Larry Chambless stands up and says to the jury, "We are here to prove within a reasonable doubt that Mrs. Eva Henderson killed her husband in cold blood, by shooting him in the back, then in the front." As he is walking back and forth in front of them. "We will present witnesses to testify, and present a video of her confession, and a signed written confession also. We will also present the 911 call from the defendant on the day of the murder." He then takes his seat.

"Is that all Mr. District Attorney?" Says the judge.

"Yes," says, Mr. Chambless.

"Is the defense ready," the judge asks, "To give your opening statement?"

"Yes, I am ready your honor." As Ms Fowler one of defense lawyers stands up and addresses the Jury. "The jury will see that my client was abused for years by her husband, and one of the reasons she turned to alcohol was to tend with the beatings, and verbal abuses. We will also provide witnesses to her defense."

"Is that all Ms. Fowler?" The judge asks.

"Yes your honor." Ms. Fowler answers.

"Prosecution you can call your first witness." Judge Bridewell states.

Assistant District Attorney Larry Chambless tells the court, "I call Johnson County Sheriff's Detective Jeff Moran to the witness stand." After being sworn in, District Attorney Chambless asks Detective Moran, "I would like you to tell the jury how you questioned Mrs. Martin in the interview room at the Johnson County Law Enforcement Center, and how you obtained the confession? and how you video-tape recorded it?"

After reading the written confession, Jeff Moran tells the District Attorney, "You can please start the video tape that was recorded now."

The Assistant District Attorney Larry Chambless stands up and turning towards the Bailiff, says, "You can start the videotape."

The Bailiff turns on the television, and starts the videotape. The videotape shows a frail looking Eva Henderson, seemingly confused, and dazed, recounting the events of that night. Eva gives Moran this account of the night her husband died.

She says, "I was at home in bed that day, trying to get over the flu, and woke up about five pm. feeling worse. I called my husband, who had left that morning to take our grandson to school, and then he went onto work. He answered the phone, and told me that he was just about to leave for home. I went back to sleep, and when my husband got home he woke me up."

"I know you haven't eaten anything for a couple of days, so I am going to fix us something to eat."

"My stomach was queasy, but I ate some of the soup he fixed, and then threw it up." Eva continues "then my husband fixed us both a drink of whiskey. As I sat down to drink it he began to berate me for staying home, and sleeping all day." On the tape, she says, "My husband called me 'lazy damn witch,' and he accused me of just wanting to get out of work, and complained that the house hadn't been cleaned. He used a number of obscenities, and called me some bad names. I drank the whiskey, and a few minutes later, I threw it up."

As the tape continues, she is saying, "I don't know how long my husband continued to harangue me, I don't remember very well." She says, "He just kept fussing, fussing, and then fussing at me some more." Finally she says, "He slapped me very hard upside on my head." She tells Moran, "I can't remember clearly what happened next. I think I walked into the bedroom, I seen a gun under the pillow, and I never seen it there before, I got the gun out from under the pillow on the bed."

As the tape continues, she says, "I went into the room where he was to show him the gun, and I see him lying on the floor. I then ran to the phone, and dialed 9-1-1, and after that I went back to my husband, and stayed with him until investigators arrived. I tried to see how bad he was, and if he was alive."

Then she tells Moran, "I do remember the police pounding on the front and back doors, but they were both locked, and they broke thru the doors, and got inside."

On the tape Moran asks several times, "Why did you get the gun?"

She appears confused, and answers, "I don't have any idea why, I just seen it there, and wanted to show it to him. One time" she says, "All he was trying to do was care for me…trying to feed me, and get me well." She says, "I love him so much, but I don't like him." Then she says, "I don't know if I'm crazy or not? I must be! I don't know?"

Detective Moran then asks Mrs. Martin, "About signing the confession?"

She breaks down again, "I can't believe all of this happening," she sobs, "I could not read it because I didn't have my glasses on, but I signed it anyway, because of the shock I was in I guess, and just trying to get this behind me."

The detective says to her, "I understand, something like this happens real quick."

The Assistant District Attorney stands up, and says, "Your honor that is all for this witness, defense your witness."

The Defense Attorney Shelly Fowler asks Detective Moran, "You told the jury that you often write out the confessions for suspects, but admitted that the tape showed Eva Henderson telling him that she had left her glasses at home, and could not see what she was signing, and also there were other instances between the written, and the tape version. Including a number of deletions, that seemed to help the prosecution. For example, Eva Henderson's statements about her husband's anger when she decided not to go to work, his calling her "lazy witch", and the use of profanity, and obscenities were all left out of the written confession, as was your remark about her husband hitting her upside of her head?"

"Yes," Moran replied.

"Mr. Moran every time Eva Henderson began to talk about her husband's abuse, you cut her short, and changed the subject?"

"I didn't realize I did that." Said Detective Moran.

"But you did, according to the tape." Then she asks the question, "Do you know what name Mrs. Henderson used for her husband?

"I believe it was Gordon," he said.

"Gordon, Detective is her oldest son's name, Noting that throughout the written confession, Mr. Henderson is referred to as "Gordon" She then states, "Eva Henderson always called her husband 'Mat'. She never said the word 'Gordon in the whole tape. These are your words aren't they Detective Moran?"

"Yes I guess so," replied detective Moran.

"This is your interpretation of what she said, and not what she actually said isn't it?" Fowler says.

"Yes I wrote it out, says the Detective.

"Judge because this statement is what the detective wrote, and not what Mrs. Henderson said, I ask that the written confession be thrown out."

"Denied," the judge says, "Because the defendant signed it, and the Jury can discuss it in their deliberation."

"That is all I have for this witness." Says Ms. Fowler. The Judge says, "The state can call their next witness."

"The prosecutions enter into evidence another tape recording, one of the 9-1-1 calls by Eva Henderson," Bill Mason the assistant D. A. says to the court, "Your honor we would like to play the tape now."

As the tape plays, "Eva is sobbing, and screaming as she tells the operator, "My husband has been shot, and he needs medical help right away." (She can be heard shouting, seemingly from the back ground) "He's not moving. My God! Please, please help him....You're not dead, you're not dead, you're not dead, wake up....please, please wake up." As the tape played one of the Martin family members got up, and walked out of the court room in tears, and one of the jurors also was visibly shaken.

After the tape finished in about ten minutes, Assistant District Attorney Bill Mason stands up, and says, I call my next witness, Medical Examiner Dr. Marie Araneta."

After the pathologist is sworn in, The DA says, "Good morning Dr. Araneta."

"Good morning to you to." answers the Dr.

Asst. D.A. Bill Mason then states, "Doctor Araneta, will you please tell the jury about the autopsy that you performed on Mr. Mathew Henderson, a few days after the shooting?"

"Mr. Henderson died from a gunshot wound that entered his left lower back, and traveled upward, and tore through his aorta artery, causing blood to gush into his chest cavity. As he fell forward, he turned over and landed on the floor on his back." Then she says, "He also suffered another gunshot wound to his left abdomen, a shot that entered through the front, and hit his liver, and lodged in the side of his chest. That wound was made by someone standing from the front and side of him, in my opinion."

Dr. Araneta continues to say, "Because of the amount of bleeding caused by the first wound, it appears the second shot did not come immediately afterward. I believe there was a little time between the two shots, because of the blood clot where the bullet was lodged, it could have been anywhere from one to three minutes." The Doctor then states, "The autopsy also revealed that Mr. Henderson had an alcohol content of .038. The legal limit is .10. Also the autopsy revealed that Mr. Henderson had no testicles, and has a 5-inch long scar from an earlier wound in the scrotum area."

"Your honor that is all the questions I have," says the prosecutor. "The defense can question this witness now."

Defense attorney Fowler stands up and goes to the podium, then says, "Dr. Araneta the preliminary report showed that the front wound may have been an exit wound."

The pathologist answers, "That didn't happen, as both bullets were found in the body."

"That's all Doctor Araneta," says Ms. Fowler"

"The state can call their next witness," the judge says to the court.

The prosecution assistant district attorney then calls Corporal Eakins of the Burleson police department. After being sworn in, the DA asks, "Corporal Eakins will you state to the jury what happened on the day you responded to the home of Mat and Eva Henderson on Jan 10th of this year."

"Officer Howard Baker, and I responded to the residence of the Henderson's to secure the scene until Johnson County deputies got there. We went to the front door, and it was locked. Officer Baker went around to the back, and found it to be locked also. We could hear a woman screeching and crying inside, both of us simultaneously kicked in both doors, and entered into the house." The deputy then says, "We found a middle-aged woman in a white robe kneeling over the victim in the living room. She was saying, 'I can't believe he's dead'. I found a revolver on a counter between the living room, and the dining room, it was a .38 caliber Smith and Wesson pistol. I dumped the ammunition out of the gun, and put the revolver back on the counter. I found three fired rounds, and three unfired rounds. I left the scene when the Johnson County deputies arrived."

Assistant district attorney then says, "Your witness," to the defense attorney.

Defense attorney Fowler stands up, and says to the witness, "Corporal Eakins, Did you think my client, whom was crying hysterically, did not open the door for the officers deliberately?"

Eakins replied, "No."

"No more questions for this witness your honor."

The prosecutions say, "Your honor we call Detective Matt Wylie of the Johnson County Sheriff's Office."

The judge says, "Bailiff please tells Detective Mat Wylie of the Johnson County Sheriff's department take the stand."

After taking the stand and being sworn in, the prosecutor says, "Detective Wylie will you tell the jury what happened at the Martin's home on Jan. 10th this year."

"When I arrived the emergency team arrived also at the same time as we found the paramedics were attempting to treat the victim. I took Mrs. Henderson to a bedroom, and called for investigators." The detective Wylie then states, "The defendant spoke coherently, and detailed the events, and appeared calmed down. I took her into the bedroom, and left as she put on some clothes, then the policeman took her to the Johnson County Jail, then Detective Bill Bailey videotaped the crime scene at 7:35p.m."

Prosecutor Bill Mason then admits the tape into evidence and asks the judge, "We would like to play the tape now, your honor."

"Bailiff, Will you please play the tape now, thank you," says the judge.

The jury then observed the tape, and some still pictures of the crime scene. The photo's showed the recliner the victim was sitting in at the time of the shooting, the revolver, and the location of one of the bullet entry wounds near the victim's naval.

After the tape plays the prosecutor says, "No more questions for this witness your honor."

The judge then says, "Your witness Ms. Fowler."

Ms. Fowler stands up, and looking directly at Det. Wylie, and says, "No questions for this witness, your honor."

Assistant District Attorney Bill Mason stands up, and says, "Your honor we call Detective Bill Bailey to the stand."

After being sworn in the District Attorney Mason says, "Detective please tell the jury about what happened at the Henderson's house on Jan. 10th 1994."

Detective Bill Bailey after being sworn it testifies, "Detective Wylie picked up the revolver from the crime scene, and secured it in his patrol unit, until I arrived at about 7:30p.m. The revolver was taken out of the patrol car, and placed on the bar where Policeman Eakins had found it for the purpose of videotaping and photographing the scene." Bailey then testifies, "A spent bullet, accounting for the third spent bullet, was found inside a room set up as an office/weight room."

"That is all for this witness," says the prosecutor then adds, "Your honor."

"Defense your witness," says the judge.

Ms. Fowler still sitting at her desk says, "No questions for this witness your honor."

"You are excused detective." Then the judge as he is standing says, "This will conclude today's calendar, and will reconvene tomorrow at 1:15p.m.

At 1:15p.m. On Wednesday the 29th of June Judge Bridewell states, "This court is now in session, and the state can call your next witness."

The prosecution as he stands up, and addresses the judge he says, "We call Robert A. Poole to the stand your honor."

Bill Mason of the prosecution asks, "Robert Poole tell the jury what your job is."

"I work for the forensic department of the Johnson County Sheriff's office," says Mr. Poole.

"And what did you find at the home of the Henderson's on Jan. 10th 1994." Prosecutor Bill Mason asks.

"I examined a .38 caliber smith & Wesson revolver that the deputies found at the residence of the Martins'. And I found that three bullets were fired from the revolver," then adds, "And Mrs. Martins finger prints on it."

"That's all for this witness." Says the prosecutor.

"Your witness Ms. Fowler." says the judge.

As the defense Attorney stands up, and walks toward the podium she says, "Mrs. Martin Henderson has stated that she picked up the gun from under a pillow in the bedroom, and carried it into the room where Mr. Henderson was, her finger prints on the gun do not prove that she fired the gun Mr. Poole, is that right?"

"Yes, I say it would not prove she fired the gun, as we could not identify the prints on the trigger." says Mr. Poole.

"That's all for this witnesses your honor." As Ms. Fowler goes over to her chair, and sat down.

At 3:00p.m. The prosecution says, "We rest our case your honor."

CHAPTER SIX

Looking at the defense table the judge says, "Defense, "you can call your first witness."

Ms. Fowler stands up and address's the court, "We call Mrs. Eva Henderson to the stand your honor."

Eva takes the stand and gets sworn in. Defense attorney Fowler says, "Mrs. Henderson tell the jury about the abuse that you took from your husband Mat Henderson."

"I believe the abuse began before Mat and I were married in 1960." Eva continues, "One time Mat yanked me off of a bar stool, and took his belt off, and whipped me right at the bar." She said, "Another time he hit, and choked me, and threatened to throw me out of a seven story window at a hotel we were staying. All because my car broke down, and the manager of the dealership the tow truck took me to, was kind enough to buy me dinner because Mat was out of town, and we had to wait for the plane to get to the airport, and that angered Mat, although he never said anything to the manager."

"On another occasion, Eva says, "He drove his pickup to where I was working, and when I came to the window with one of the workers, he waved a gun at me, scaring the other woman, but I wasn't scared as he thought I would be, and left without any more incident."

"Another time I left work, and went out with some co-worker friends, and when I got home, Ed grabbed me by my clothes, and tore them down to my waist, then knocked me to the floor, and kicked me with his steel toed boots, my two sons were looking on. My youngest son Martin, told his dad not to hit me anymore, Mat got a look on his face like someone threw ice water on it, and he left the room."

Eva goes on with another abusive incident, "In 1975 I was going to leave him, and go to Houston Texas, but when I was getting ready to leave he shows up, and apparently had been drinking, he comes into the house, and hits me right in the face, knocking me down, and I slid all the way down the hall, and over a chair. He went into the kitchen and made himself a drink, then came into the room I was in, and after some words, he threw the drink in my face glass and all. I rubbed my face where he hit me, and I could see blood on my hand, and it was running down my arm, I thought he was going to kill me. He went back into the kitchen, and made himself another drink, and I went into the boy's bedroom, and took down a shotgun from the rack my son Gordon made, and opened a drawer and took out a shell, and put it in, and I was surprised that it fit.

When he came into the room he was yelling bad names, and was really angry, I pointed the gun at him, and told him to stop, but he kept coming so I pulled the trigger. The shell hit him in the groin, and he ended up losing his testicles." Hal never filed charges, but I left and went to Los Angeles with my sister, then I went to Houston."

As she continues, "I admit being an alcoholic, and I thought Hal was one too. But he claimed that he wasn't, he was a man that would make me beg for some alcohol, that he had locked up in a safe. I loved him, but I didn't like him."

Shelly Fowler her court appointed defense lawyer says, "What about the incident on Jan. 10, 1994?

"I don't remember firing the gun," says Eva, "I remember going into the room where he was, and seeing him lying there."

After about one and a half hours of testimony, Ms. Fowler says to the judge, "I am through with this witness."

"Your witness Mr. Prosecutor," says the judge.

The District Attorney stands up and says to the court, "No questions your honor."

"You can call your next witness Ms. Fowler," says the Judge. "Defense will call Dr. Finn she is a doctor of Psychiatry to the stand."

"Bailiff," says the judge, "Please call Dr. Finn to the witness stand and swear her in."

After being sworn in, Ms. Fowler asks Dr. Finn, "Did you interview Mrs. Martin?"

"Yes," doctor Finn replies, "In fact I interviewed her twice."

"After the two interviews," Ms. Fowler says, "What did you feel about Mrs. Henderson?"

"I feel like Mrs. Henderson was or is an alcoholic, habitually depressed, and suffering from the battered wife syndrome (Post Traumatic Stress)."

"On January 10," asks Ms. Fowler, "And the shooting of Mr. Henderson, did Mrs. Henderson say anything?"

"Mrs. Henderson as she came out of the bedroom she was in, and entered into the hall way," says Dr. Finn, "She described seeing someone kneeling over her husband's body. But being an alcoholic, and having post-traumatic stress syndrome, she could have been hallucinating.

"Could Mrs. Henderson actually have seen someone?"

"Yes I guess she could have, but as far as we know there was no one else in the house at that time."

"Is it not possible that someone with a key could have come into the house, shot Mr. Henderson, go into the bedroom, and leave the pistol under the pillow, without Mrs. Henderson seeing or hearing him, and then leave the house, and locking the door behind him or her.? Says Ms. Fowler.

"That is possible," says Dr. Finn, "I suppose that could have happened."

Ms. Fowler says, "Did she hallucinate about anything else?" Ms. Fowler asks.

"No I do not recall of her saying that."

Your witness Mr. Prosecutor." As Ms. Fowler sits down.

"Dr. Finn I agree with you that someone could have come in, and all that the defense said, but there is no evidence that, that happened is there." said the prosecutor.

Dr. Finn says, "Not as far as I can recall."

Assistant District Attorney Mason asks, "Dr. Finn, was the shooting an intentional act?"

"Possibly," says Dr. Finn, "Since the gun was in another room before the shooting occurred." And adding, "There is often associated with years of abuse that an explosive violent release, that might require some fore thought."

"That's all Dr. Finn, you are excused." District attorney Mason says.

As Dr. Finn leaves the witness stand, Judge Bridewell looks at, and says to Ms. Fowler, "Call your next witness."

Fowler stands up, and says to the court, "Your Honor, the Defense calls Edith Sparks to the witness stand your Honor."

After Edith Sparks takes the stand, and gets sworn in, Ms. Fowler says, "Edith you are the sister of Mrs. Henderson is that correct."

"Yes that is correct."

"Mrs. Sparks, How did you and Mr. Henderson get along?"

"At first when they lived in South Carolina, he was a good and happy man," said Edith, "But when they moved to Texas, he changed a lot. Every time I would visit them, he always looked, and acted unhappy, and I became afraid of him."

"Your witness Mr. Prosecutor." Says the Defense attorney.

Mr. Mason asks "Have you ever seen any abuse from Mr. Henderson to Mrs. Henderson on your visits to them?"

"I never witnessed any abuse, but the tension was always there, Eva would never say anything or do anything that might make him angry, or upset."

"So as far as you know or witnessed there was no abuse."

"No."

"Your honor that is all for this witness."

Judge Bridewell says, "Ms. Fowler call your next witness."

"Your honor the defense rests our case." Stated Ms. Fowler.

"Mr. Prosecutor do you have any rebuttal witnesses?"

"Yes your honor, we have six more witnesses. Our first witness is Johnson County's Deputy Sheriff Corporal Jerry W. Scarborough."

Judge Bridewell says to the court, "Will Sheriff Deputy Corporal Jerry W. Scarborough please takes the stand."

Jerry Scarborough takes the stand and gets sworn in. Prosecutor Mr. Mason asks, "Tell the Jury about your calls to the Henderson's house, before the shooting."

Deputy Scarborough says to the Jury, "My department called me out to the Henderson's house on East Bethesda Road at least five times. One report includes claims by Mrs. Henderson that Mr. Henderson was denying her food, and her medications, after looking around, I became aware that the medications were readily available, and there was plenty of food around for her to eat. On another report, Mrs. Henderson stated that Mr. Henderson had assaulted her, but Mr. Henderson was out of town at the time. Another report states that Mrs. Henderson called and said she was assaulted, but Mr. Henderson was not there. Mrs. Henderson on at least three of the calls appeared intoxicated or had alcohol on her breath. On another report I went out to the house, and the allegations were unfounded."

Prosecutor Mason says, "That's all your witness."

Defense attorney Ms. Fowler says, Deputy Scarborough on some of those reports, could the victim Mr. Henderson left the premises before you got there?"

Deputy Scarborough says, "Yes I presume it could have happened, but nothing was said so I didn't put it in my report."

Ms. Fowler says, "So then Mrs. Henderson's allegations could have been correct."

Deputy Scarborough says, "In that case yes."

Ms. Fowler says, "Judge that's all for this witness."

Judge Bridewell says, "Prosecution calls your next witness."

Prosecutor Mason says, "We call Mrs. Thelma Martin Tracey to the stand, your Honor."

After Mrs. Tracey was sworn in, Mr. Mason says, "Being Mr. Henderson's Sister, and we know that the Henderson's were married for a long time, and I am sure that you were close to them, so Mrs. Tracey, do you know about any abuse to Mrs. Henderson from your brother Mathew Henderson?"

"I lived with the two of them in South Carolina, and also when we all moved to Texas. All of this time I never witnessed any abuse from my brother towards Eva, and my brother treated her like a queen, and that to me I feel is what every woman would relish."

"In reference to the 1975 shooting of your brother Mr. Henderson, do you have anything to say?" asks the DA.

Mrs. Tracey says, "Mrs. Henderson called me and said," 'I finally shot him, and if you want to see him alive you better head to John Peter Smith Hospital," Mrs. Tracey continues, "Mat had a hard time with that but did survive, and never filed anything against her for shooting him."

"Judge Bridewell that is all for this witness." "Ms. Fowler your witness." says the judge.

Mrs. Tracey, do you know why Mrs. Henderson shot your brother in 1975? Asks Ms. Fowler?"

Mrs. Tracey answers, "Yes, she said that he was drinking, and was quite inebriated, and was threatening, and hitting on her, so she was defending herself."

Ms. Fowler asks, "Do you know why your brother Mr. Henderson didn't leave Mrs. Henderson after the 1975 shooting."

Mrs. Tracey answers, "He told me somebody needed to take care of her."

Ms. Fowler says, "That's all the questions I have for this witness, your Honor." Ms. Fowler says."

"Mr. Mason call your next witness."

"Prosecution calls Mrs. Len Hirst to the stand."

"Bailiff call Mrs. Len Hirst to the stand." says the judge.

After Mrs. Hirst was sworn in Mr. Mason says to her, "Mrs. Hirst how did you know the defendant Mrs. Henderson?"

"I was a co-worker and a friend" said Mrs. Hirst.

"Tell the jury how Mr. Henderson treated Mrs. Henderson." says the DA.

Mrs. Hirst answers, "Mr. Henderson treated Mrs. Henderson very loving, and considerate."

"That's all, your witness Ms. Fowler."

No questions for this witness, your Honor." says Mrs. Fowler.

"Your Honor we call Ms. Ruth Wenzel to the stand."

After being sworn in, Mr. Mason says, "Ms. Wenzel how did you know the defendant Mrs. Henderson?"

"I had lived with them for six months in 1992, and I considered the two of them like parents, and all this time I never saw any abuse." Says Ruth. "Mrs. Henderson would tell me everything, if she was abused she would have told me, and I would have seen any bruises. Mrs. Henderson called me on Jan.10 th 1994 after the shooting, and she said she was tired of him, and that it seemed like the thing to do."

"Your Honor that is all for this witness." says the DA. "Ms. Fowler do you have any questions for this witness?"

"Yes you're Honor, Ms. Wenzel, do you recall an incident at work with Mrs. Henderson, as she was sitting in front of the window, and Mr. Henderson drives up in his pickup truck, and brandishes a hand gun, and points it at Mrs. Henderson.

"Yes I recall that incident, but Mr. Henderson did not point it at anyone, he just drove off."

"You don't think that he was trying to intimidate, or scare Mrs. Henderson with the hand gun, you think it is alright to wave a gun at someone, and not mean anything by it."

"Well I remember I was quite scared, but not Mrs. Henderson she just turned to me, and said it's alright he was just showing off."

"You testified that Mrs. Hendersonin called you after the shooting, my question is how long after the shooting did she call you?"

"Well it must have been a few days, I think."

Ms. Fowler says, "That's all for this witness, your Honor."

Call your next witness, Mr. Mason" says the judge.

"We call Billy Bethel to the stand your Honor." says Mr. Mason.

Billy Bethel gets sworn in, and Mr. Mason asks, "What is your relationship with Mrs.Henderson, Billy?"

Billy answers, "I am the grandson of Mrs. Henderson they adopted me when my mother disappeared, when I was four years old up to my sixteenth year."

Assistant District Attorney Mason asks, "During these twelve years, was there a lot of abuse from your step grandfather Henderson towards your grandmother Eva."

"No, all the time I lived with them, I never seen any abuse between my step grandfather, and my grandmother."

"That's all for this witnesses your Honor." "Your witness Ms. Stuebing." says the judge.

Defense Attorney Sybil Stuebing says, "Billy why did you leave at the age of sixteen."

Billy states, "I didn't like it when my grandmother, and step grandfather split up and my grandmother moved to Houston to live by herself, and she wouldn't take me with her."

Ms. Stuebing says, "Were you angry enough to turn against her now, after she had been so good to you, taking you in for 12 years."

"I am not angry, and I am just telling you the truth." Billy answered.

Ms. Stuebing says, to the judge, "That's all for this witnesses your Honor."

Mr. Mason stands up and says, "We rest our case your Honor." "Does the Defense have any rebuttal witnesses?"

Ms. Fowler stands up and says, "We do your Honor, we call Eudora Boutwell to the stand."

Ms. Boutwell was sworn in and Defense Attorney Fowler says, "What is your relationship with Mrs. Martin?"

"I am a very close friend, and I know her enough to say it wouldn't surprise me if no one but herself knew of the reported abuse. You don't tell things like that, she would never do that."

Ms. Fowler said, "That's all your witness."

Assistant District Attorney Mason stands up and says, "No questions you're Honor."

Ms. Fowler stands up and says, "Defense rests your Honor."

"Time for closing arguments," says Judge Bridewell, "Go ahead Mr. Mason."

After both sides gave their closing arguments, the judge says, "The Jury is now excused for deliberation."

On Thursday June 30, 1994 at 5:30pm the jury came into the court room with a verdict after only twenty five minutes of deliberating, and after leaving the court room. The judge read the guilty verdict at 5:36 pm... Eddie hearing the verdict dabbed at her eyes as her family cried. Family and friends of the victim, 69 year old Mathew Henderson. Quietly celebrated. After three days of testimony and closing arguments, the nine men, and three woman, jury, deliberated at 5:05pm the judge recessed the jury until Friday at 9:00am for the punishment phase of the trial.

Eddie is thinking back to that time, when she was sentenced. "My friends and family were crushed. They rushed me, and hugged me. My brother whom I don't recall ever hugging me, broke through, and grabbed me, and gave me a big bear hug. I don't know if the officer with me allowed this, or my family just overwhelmed him. We are not a touch, and feel y family. I said it was almost worth the sentence to get that hug. Then the officer took me back to the jail, I was in a daze, and began making peace with god, and getting ready to come back on Friday for the punishment phase. And then start serving my sentence."

Shelly Fowler and Sybil Stuebing as they were leaving the court room, Sybil says, "I know we were looking for a different outcome."

Shelly Fowler says, "You know what Sybil, the problem I had with the verdict is that they had a 13-page charge and they came back in twenty-five minutes. It appears to me that they didn't take the time to read the charge or listen to the attorney's arguments. That really concerns me and makes me think there's a flaw in our criminal justice system."

On Friday morning at 9:00am Judge Bridewell says, "This phase of the trial is to determine the sentence for Mrs. Martin." He turned towards the jury and says, "You the jury have four options to consider,

Number one is: Life in prison plus a fine of "x" dollars.

Number two option is: "X" years in prison and a fine of "x" dollars.

Number three option is: "X" years in prison and a fine of "x dollars with the prison term being probated.

Number four option is: A probated sentence of both "x" years in prison and a fine of "x" dollars."

The judge then asked the district attorney, "Do you have any statements?"

Assistant District Attorney says, "Yes your Honor, we ask for prison time for Mrs. Martin, we feel this case calls for a penitentiary sentence."

"Do you have any comments Ms. Fowler?"

"Your Honor I ask the jury to give Mrs. Martin a probated sentence, one of the four options, I think any prison time is excessive." Then she says, "Your Honor we have three witnesses today for Mrs. Martin."

"Okay bring on your first witness."

"Our first witness is Ms. Alice Horner your Honor."

"Fine, "Says the judge, will Ms. Horner please take the stand."

Ms. Horner says, "Your Honor, I know that Mrs. Martin had attended every Alcoholics Anonymous meeting (twice a week) since she was incarcerated and that she was an active participant in those meetings."

Ms. Fowler says, "My next witness is Johnson County Law Enforcement Center Correctional Officer Toni Prine."

"Okay will Officer Toni Prine please take the Stand? Judge Bridewell states."

"When the jury gave the guilty sentence I cried, and I describe Mrs. Martin as a 'Surrogate mother' says Toni, "To the younger female inmates, she has been pleasant, respectful, and never caused any trouble in the last one hundred and seventy days."

"Your Honor our last witness is Alice Finley a community supervision officer in the adult probation dept. for Johnson County."

"Please take the stand Ms. Alice Finley." says the judge.

Alice Finley says after she takes the stand, "As a condition of probation, Mrs. Martin could be ordered to attend substance abuse classes, and submit to random urinalysis to test for alcohol use. Other options would be to affix a lock on her vehicle that would prohibit her from driving until she passes a breathalyzer test." Then Ms. Finley describes the breathalyzer device. "The device is hooked up to a television screen, so Mrs. Martin could be monitored."

Both the prosecution and defense attorneys rested their cases in the punishment phase at 10:20am respectively, Friday morning. Judge Bridewell excused the jury for deliberation at 10:35am. After 45 minutes the Jury came back into the court room. The Judge asks the jury, "Mr. Foreman of the Jury do you have a unanimous verdict?"

The Foreman says, "Yes we have your Honor, the verdict is the second choice 20 years in prison with no probation."

Later on in Eddie's cell, she was weeping and thinking, my lawyer quit my case when I talked to another attorney about doing my appeal pro-boon, but the judge refused to appoint me anther attorney, but he told my trial attorney to file my appeal, which she didn't do. The judge had to do it himself. Then after all that he appointed me another attorney to represent me, the appeal did not do anything."

CHAPTER SEVEN

Later they put Eva on a bus, and transported her to Neal prison in Amarillo, Texas. A lot of the things that went on in the prison at Neal is why she didn't like it there. After an eight and a half hour ride, I stepped off of the bus, and I was really feeling tired, and being handcuffed to another inmate was not that all pleasing either. Just for that reason alone, I made up my mind to start exercising to make myself strong; as you have to carry your own bag wherever you go. When you go place to place you pack up all your stuff, and put it in chain bags, and carry the bag, sometimes it could be even a half of a mile. When going in for the first time, I was scared silly seeing women that were huge, mostly black, and they looked more like men than men. I had never been around many of them before.

I was assigned to a cell with another inmate, and at Neal it is very violent there. At first I didn't dare to leave my cell, so I mostly lived in my cell. Talk about reality school, I didn't understand most of what was going on in there, most of the time I couldn't understand what they were saying for the most part. I told them I didn't speak their language. Thank God, they thought that was funny.

I see more blood, and gore at Neal, than when I was working as a nurse. There were fights everywhere, and they were not playing, they hit each other with metal combination locks placed in a sock, (it's made like a sap, or a blackjack) they burn each other with their curling irons, coffee pots, scolding water, and hit each other with mops, and broom handles, metal waste baskets. Inmates were fighting, and pounding heads into walls, and floors. I never left my cell, or cubicle without asking the lord's protection, and I was never bothered, although I've dodged fights in the showers, and day room, and even in the church.

At Neal prison I never seen such things that were going on there, I didn't even know that some existed. That was a reality check; some of the guards used stun guns, until a man was killed with one, in one of the men's unit, and later the stun guns were outlawed and abandoned. The officer's would body slam women right and left, officers themselves were beaten up. It was a real education.

Neal was terrible, there was violence everywhere. For services rendered the inmates received jewelry, clothes, perfume, tobacco; anything else they wanted was brought in to them by officers, or anyone else that comes in from the outside. Guards even walked other officers off the unit on a daily basis. Even one of the Lieutenant's was involved.

About a year or so later, on one day early in the morning a guard came to Eddie's cell, and said, "Martin, come with me, we are going to the laundry department." She didn't know why at the time, and she had no choice, but she had to go.

Arriving at the Laundry, the person in charge of the Laundry department, (the inmates called the boss) said to Eva, "Martin we are going to measure you for some Civilian Clothes."

Eva says, "Why are you measuring me for Civilian Clothes?"

The Boss said, "For unknown reasons, they are sending you to a Half-way House in Bridgeport." Then she said, "You are to be there for six months, then you will be paroled."

Eva is thinking, "I am flabbergasted," and said, "Are you sure it is me, because I have been here in prison for only a year, and I have a twenty year sentence?"

The boss says, "Okay, I will call and see if we got the right person." The boss then picks up the phone and dials the number of the person in charge of the transfer. The boss says into the phone, "This is Laundry, Can you confirm that we have the right person." Then she says into the phone, "The name is Martin, 693926, and she is here to be measured for Civilian Clothes, and they are sending her to a half-way house." After a pause, she hangs up the phone, and says to Martin, **"Yep that is you, so let's get going!"**

Eva is thinking to herself, "I cannot believe it."

Sunday night one of the officers came to her cell, and said, "Martin get your things together, and pack up, you are leaving in the morning." After breakfast, the officer came to her cell, and handcuffed her to another inmate that was also going to the halfway house. Then Eva with her free hand carried her chain bag. The officer escorted Eva and the other inmate to where the bus was waiting.

After a couple of hours, one of the officers in charge of the bus, came back to where Eva is, and says, "Martin we have a woman prisoner with a heart problem on board the bus, and knowing you are a nurse, and have worked in hospitals, and the infirmary, we want you to keep an eye on her."

Eva answers, "Oh sure, and what am I supposed to do if she arrests?" as she is thinking, "I guess all I can do is pray, if I don't do it I can get a failure to obey an order." Eva and the girl she is handcuffed to, go with the officer, and watched over the inmate until the bus arrived at Gatesville prison, about six hours later.

The bus arrives at the reception area at Gatesville prison near Waco TX. The woman with the heart problem, did not have any more problems, Eva says to herself, "Thank you God for answering my prayers." All the inmates stayed for two days, and after the two days, all of the prisoners that came together except Eva, were loaded onto the bus. After the bus was loaded, it left for the Bridgeport half-way house.

"I am left here, and I am crushed, nobody has told me anything. As I am crying, I start praying, and crying and praying, I guess I was so pitiful, that one of the guards, went to my property, and brought me my cross and my bible. I am in a cell all by myself at this time, and so I started to read the bible. I am thinking, and praying all the time that I am not going back to Neal Prison."

After a week, and on Monday, they put another girl in the cell with Eva. The other girl is coming back from a bench warrant, and she will be going back to Neal with Eva.

On Tuesday a guard came to the cell, and told them, "Pack up, and get ready to leave."

The two of them pack up, and as the guard came, she escorted them to the terrace for breakfast, and after they ate, they were taken to the bus area to be loaded onto the bus. When the bus came, the guard tells them, "The paper work isn't right, and I am taking you both back to the cell." They did this on Wednesday, and Thursday, and never put them on the bus.

On Tuesday the next week, the guard escorts both of them to the bus, but neither of them was put on it. Eva at this time is thinking, "Something is not right," and starts praying." After praying Eva is thinking, "The other girl sharing the cell with me is getting mad at me, for her being treated this way."

"It is because of you they are treating me this way," she says, "And not putting us on the bus."

"I don't know why they are doing this, it is not my fault." And she starts reading the bible again. All of a sudden she says, "It just hit me like a ton of bricks; I just read Mathew chapter twenty six, verse thirty nine; I have been praying for my will to be done, not God's." She sits down on the bed, and starts praying, "Lord I need you to be with me, and help me, only if it is your will, not mine."

When the next bus came for Amarillo Texas, Eva, and her cell mate were on the bus. When they got back to Neal, the Sergeant come up to Eva and says, "Martin, you are not staying here, you are being bench warranted to Johnson County." Then she said, "Come on we are going to the car that is going to take you."

Eva says, "We are going by car "! Not on a bus!" Then she says as she is looking to where the car is, "I see two male officers there," and she turns toward the Sergeant, and says, "I thought the process called for a female to accompany me."

The Sergeant says, "Don't worry about it. The one in charge is a Lieutenant."

The Lieutenant come over to where Eva and the Sergeant is, and he removes the handcuffs from her, and says, "Get in the car."

She says, "Okay, no problem," she is thinking, "I don't need any problem from the lieutenant," so she gets into the backseat of the police car.

Amarillo to Fort Worth in Johnson County is about a seven and a half hour ride. As they are driving along the highway, the officer driving the car pulls into a driveway to a hamburger place. The lieutenant says, "We are going to stop and get something to eat, as we haven't eaten since this morning, and if you would like a hamburger, and some French fries, I will bring them back for you."

Eva says, "Yes of course I would, I haven't had anything but prison food for a long time."

The officer's come back, and the lieutenant hands her a bag with some food, and a drink, and they get back on the road, and Eva is eating her cheeseburger, and fries, and she is thinking, "This trip is very nice, riding in a car instead of a bus, and not being handcuffed, and eating a hamburger, and fries, this I will savor."

It was around five o' clock in the afternoon when they arrived in Cleburne, in Johnson County. Eva asks the Lieutenant, "Do you think it would be possible for me to call Eudora, a good friend of mine to tell her I am in town?"

The Lieutenant answers, "Sure it would be okay, if you call her collect."

She picks up the phone, and dials Eudora's phone number, and Eudora answers, "Hello, yes I accept the charges, Eva it is you, how are you? And where are you?"

Eva answers, "Hi Eudora, I am fine, and I am here on a bench warrant in Cleburne, I have to go to court tomorrow."

Eudora answers, "Oh excellent, I will be there to see you." On the next day of her court appearance, the Lieutenant escorts Eddie to the court house. When they get there, she enters into the court room, and she sees Eudora, and her daughter Carrie, and a big smile came on Eva's face. When the judge called her case, she found out that it was not about her murder case, but about the property that was in probate court. The property is in Mat's estate, and is in Mat's name, and Eva was trying not to lose it in probate court. She has been fighting for the property since Mat died. Karla had been making payments on the property, because she was living there, also so the family would not lose it. Not knowing that the taxes were not included in the mortgage payments; the state took over for the property for non-payment of the taxes. Eva told Karla not to pay for it, as nobody had paid the taxes for over a year.

"But I have lost it all but two acres. I tried to tell them that the property was a homestead, and should not have been considered part of his estate. The property was supposed to be turned over to the heirs that included: Eva, her son Gordon, whom is in prison for messing with a sixteen year old girl, and her grandson Mickey. But the court held it up until the time run out, and the property was in too bad of shape to sell it.

It made me angry thinking about the way they handled the case, and I think that they (the probate court) stole it. The money that they got for it would not even pay off the loan we had taken out for improvements, and some finishing work, the loan was for fifty thousand dollars, and the property at that time was worth one hundred and twenty five thousand dollars."

The Probate court finished after three days, and Eva was taken back to jail in Johnson County, the Lieutenant was accompanied with a real nice female sergeant Eva knew before when she was in court for murder. The sergeant did not escort prisoners usually, but she testified at Eva's punishment phase of the trial, and she tried to get her probation. Before they left Johnson County court house, the Sergeant went with Eva to a talk to a Judge for Eva *not* to be sent back to Neal. As Eva is thinking, "It didn't work, but the sergeant, bless her heart, tried very hard." The Judge sent Eva back to Neal.

When in route with the Lieutenant, and the Sergeant, the Lieutenant said to Eva, "When we first started out, and because of your name Eva, we thought you were a man, so that is why the other officer, being a man was sent with me, but when we go back to Neal, the female sergeant will go with us. Then when we left to get you nobody knew where you were. I called TDC, and was told me you were in Bridgeport, and as we were driving there, I called Bridgeport, and they told me you were not there. We turned around and went back to Johnson County for new paper work. When we got the new paper work, we left for Neal, and finally caught up with you."

Eva is thinking, "I never have discovered why all this happened, it must have been because of all the prayers that I made to God."

After they arrived at Neal, and everything settled down for Eva, things seemed to change for the good. She met some inmates, and became friends with them. All of the friends she met would volunteer to do something for her, like: Wash her clothes, fix her hair, cook for her, and help her with her legal work on her case. Eva also had a great job in the infirmary, and a young boss who treated her like his grandmother, or mom. He was a sweetheart, and a real cutie. All the inmates and officers loved him.

A year later Neal prison was turned over completely to the men, and they sent all of the women to Gatesville prison near Waco Texas.

CHAPTER EIGHT

All the women at Neal Prison were bussed to Gatesville Prison. After they got settled in we were assigned to a cubicle, and not a cell. Most cubicles had at least ten inmates.

There were a lot of good things that happened to me, and a lot of bad things, but looking back now I can see the Lord blessed me, and still is, with the best of everything I messed up. It's a shame I couldn't see then what I do now, that's one good thing that prison does for you, (if there is anything good about prison) if you really want to get answers, and improve your life. You have time to really do some thinking, and dig out all the problems, and mistakes. But you have to be willing, and strong enough to take the responsibility of admitting to all the things you've done, and take the blame, and deal with all the pain.

I couldn't do it on my own, and I don't think many people can, without the Lord to give them the strength, and courage. I've always doubted that anyone can be helped with addiction, or any behavior problems until they admit to the problem, and dig it out, then deal with it. Most people can't or won't deal with their problems without the Lord's help. That's where my son Carl is, and my husband was. Neither of them would admit, and accept responsibility for their actions, and I wouldn't either, until I got to prison, and accepted the Lord in my life.

Thinking back on prison life; the worse part has not been dealing with the other inmates, but actually the Lord has blessed me in that. I have had only a few problems with other inmates, and ended up friends with most of them. Actually I have made a lot of friends in here in spite of the age gap. The biggest thing is that most of the women— bless their hearts, have little self-esteem, and have suffered abuse that I haven't even thought of. Some of them are people pleasers, or they want to control me. I react very badly to someone trying to control me because of my abuse history, and because of that I have become very independent, so when someone tries to care for me (so to speak) I resent it.

I have had to do some adjusting, because my 'Hearing' has become quite a problem, and I have to depend on someone else. This problem I have with my hearing sometimes makes me very angry, and unfortunately I will take it out on anyone that is handy at that moment. I have been blessed that most of the people involved with me being angry, will usually overlook it, and love me anyway, as I will apologize later.

I am a firm believer in the fact, that if you don't use it, you will lose it. I will remain active as long as possible. Right now I take no medications, I don't smoke, and I exercise every day. The only thing that stops me right now is the allergies that I have acquired since I have been in prison. It seems that I developed the 'Hives', and other allergies. I itched so bad and scratched until I cried, I couldn't get any medication, or any medical help of any kind. I kept trying to get medical help, until finally; I got to see a Doctor. She apologized when she seen me, because of all the sores that were all over my body.

The Nurse Practitioner said to me, "You are Hyper allergic to everything."

I told her, "No I am not, I am just allergic to prison, as I never had any of these problems before I got here." They still wouldn't send me home.

"The really main problem is the lack of anything mentally stimulating to do, except: reading books, or writing, or reading letters, that of which I do a lot of. When I first arrived here at Gatesville prison, I found out that there were a few classes offered for anyone. One being for self- improvement I started taking the class's one-at -a-time, until I had taken them all. Second were bible studies on religion, and I became a firm believer in the word.

After the classes I started to go to the Library, and work on my case, and study my bible. I would leave my house after breakfast then as soon as I could I would go and stay at the Library until lunch time. After lunch I would then go back to the library until supper time. After supper time, I would then go back to the library, and leave just before lights out at night. This went on until I had gone over all of my case.

All the time I had been there I never seen any women having sex openly, until one morning I got up around five thirty AM., the lights came on at four thirty AM., and started to go towards the restroom, I seen other people walking around, I don't know where the officer was. I looked across the aisle and seen one women sitting on the edge of her bunk with her legs spread open, and another woman kneeling down on her knees, with her head between the legs of the woman sitting on the bunk, doing her thing. If they would have put a sheet or blanket over themselves I would not have seen them, but I could not avoid seeing them, as my mouth dropped open, and I was in shock for a few seconds.

I reported this to the Officer, and the Chaplain, and all they said was, "So sorry, but an organization called 'Safe Prison' won't let us do anything about that."

I said to the Lieutenant, "I want to be moved to another cubicle."

The Lieutenant said, "It won't make any difference, as they do it over there also."

So far nothing has been done, and I have been praying a lot more for these women in here. I've said, "It's like living in a kennel full of females in heat." This is almost as bad as Neal."

I had one big Black Guard who intimidated me, and took a dislike to me from the first time I met her, and for quite a while. She made my life miserable for years. One day I finally got mad enough to disrespect her, and said, "I don't like the way you have treated me over the years, and I am going to turn you in." I wrote her up a couple of times, and after that there were no more problems. I am thinking that was about the worst part of the time I have been in prison.

There were times like—when we were not in the cubicle, and were being escorted by officers, and the officers humiliated me by not letting me go to the restroom until I could not hold it any longer, and peed on myself, while all the other inmates in the group were watching. But in all cases the inmates rallied to my defense on my behalf, and took up for me, and took care of me, because of my age. Most of the inmates called me Grandma.

As I am thinking back, I remember a time when a Hispanic woman was put in my cubical, and we got on each other's nerves really bad, and almost came to blows. She was thirty nine years old, and had been in prison for nineteen years. When I moved into the area in the bed next to Her, She decided to treat me as she did, or seem to do, to the others living next to her. Well I refused to be intimidated by Her, and She did some evil things, such as: She threw my underwear in the trash— accusing me of leaving tooth paste in the sink—She complained if I ate fish (Mackerel) because it smelled bad, so she turned out the lights whenever I was reading—finally, she stole my ID card that we had to wear around our neck, (nothing was done about that either) that was when we almost came to blows, but I did tell her what an evil person she was. I never did understand why my prayers weren't answered about her. Then again I think it was answered at Christmas time as the inmate in question came up to me, and gave me a big hug, (and She is not the hugging type). Oh!!—I was moved away from her area back in June.

I had been at Gatesville prison for about six years, when my sister Edith visited me, and she told me my son Gordon was in prison for messing with a sixteen year old girl. Edith gave me his address, and I wrote him a letter. He wrote me, "I am sorry for not being there for you, and I do not blame you for what happened".

"Growing up, Gordon never spent a lot of time with me, although we did have a relationship, except always disagreeing about a lot of things, just like his dad. I said He turned himself into a carbon copy of his dad, trying to earn his dad's love, and respect. Didn't work of course, just like my efforts never worked. Now that he is in prison, he did an about face, and now is able to see his dad as he was, which hasn't helped him, or his mental outlook at all.

He's more messed up now than ever, and I, like a dummy try to make him see the light. That's not going to work in prison, any more than it did outside of prison. We keep fighting just like his dad and I did. It just hit me, just how stupid that is.

The law says that we can meet another inmate one time a year for two hours. It was set up for me to be bussed to Hughes Unit, a man's unit just a few miles from Gatesville prison. We haven't had another meeting together for two years. To get visits, and almost anything else, you have to be case free, and etc. My first impression was how much Gordon had aged, but he was still in good physical condition with huge bicep muscles, a guy's thing in prison. Working out, and getting tattoos, which He had a bunch of new ones? of which did not please me, we talked a lot about what happened, how we felt about our family, and a lot of things; it was nice.

The next time I met Him, I was on crutches, from having knee surgery. I tore the misusages loose in my knee exercising. I was on crutches or a cane for six months, before, and after surgery. That visit was pretty much like the first one, except he had built up some new muscles; of course he had to show them off. I guess the visit went well, because we were supervised, and had to be nice. But we still fight in letters, as I get very angry that he won't grow up, and do what I want him to do, like act with some sense. He will never get out of prison acting the way he keeps getting into trouble, and is getting cases hand over fist, and getting put in solitary confinement, I have never been in there, and don't want to, as I am getting close to serving my time, and I don't need any more problems.

Even if he gets a chance at parole, or anything else, and things change all the time, He would not have a prayer with all the trouble he's been in. I will do everything in my power to help him get out of prison, I am praying for Gordon, and trying my best not to worry like a mother, it doesn't do any good, but it is making me grayer.

Looking back in the years, and realizing that I have done a lot of nursing care in here, but I don't anymore. I came to an abrupt halt, after spending some time trying to stop a gal from bleeding out; then I found out the next day that she was HIV positive; fortunately for me I wore rubber gloves, and was not infected. I remember that it takes medical from fifteen to twenty minutes or longer to respond to a call from a dorm., and if it's after infirmary hours, no telling how long it would take for them to get there.

All this thinking reminds me of a little lady in here, she was seventy years old when she got here, and has a twenty year sentence for driving while drinking, and hit a Child. Anyways she was a spunky little thing, and she started feeling really bad. A few days of that, and I knew she was seriously ill. So I argued with the officer, and finally he called medical, and I got her dressed, and we had to drag her up to the infirmary. She protested all the way there, the nurse checked her over, and then called for an ambulance. At the hospital, the surgeon put in a Pace Maker for her, and when she returned, she looked as good as before all that happened".

"I have been in here now for eighteen years, and I put in for parole, the last time they voted for me was two years ago. Before they will consider you, you are required to take the 'Change classes,' to help you re-orientate yourself into society, that didn't happen two years ago. I haven't met with the parole board as yet but suddenly I am in change classes. Evidently parole has already decided to let me go, and will let me know sometime in the future, or if ever. They have been known to just push you right out the gate without a word.

The classes last about three months, or one hundred eighty hours class time. The school has a two week summer vacation so that pushes everything up. I am not used to sitting in a class for three or more hours at a time. It is very tiring, especially since I'm straining to hear everything going on, as I think I am going deaf. I have to go to the Ear-nose-throat specialist, and once starting that, begins a snowball effect of tests. So I've been running here, and there, and that can get very complicated in here.

When you get a pass that may say one time on it, the time passes, and you end up waiting for two to three hours, and sometimes you have to leave the unit, and go somewhere outside the unit. That means you could be waiting or sitting out in the cold wet whatever, waiting for transportation.

And that could go for returning also, you may have to wait or even spend hours waiting for a ride back to the unit, then of course we have to be stripped, and searched each time we leave one place, and go to another. (That is if you go off unit.) This tells me I am getting too old for all this activity, I may have plenty of energy for interesting, and fun activities, and at least I hope I will. It would be a real shame to wait all these years to get back into the world, and then not being able to enjoy it.

All of this going here and there came down came onto me at once, and I am still reeling, but I'm hoping things will slow down some now, and I'll be able to catch my breath, and adjust to some sort of routine, and I won't be laid out in lavender all the time. (I heard that expression somewhere before.)

I should be hearing from the parole board one way or the other soon, because an inmate Jennifer, here in the dorm is having her husband check with the parole board about my statist. The last time she talked to him, he said they were voting on me, so I should be hearing from them soon.

I should be out of my change classes in about two weeks. It can't be too soon for me. That class is really kicking my behind. After all this I have to find a sponsor that will help me once I get out. They gave me a list of sponsor's and I wrote to them, one at a time, now I have to wait until I get an answer. Jennifer's husband visited her, and told her I got my parole. When she came to me, she was so excited she was jumping up and down. She told me I was getting an FI-1, which is an immediate release, or as immediate as it gets, here T.D.C., I didn't want it told around, as I had enough going on without all of the hoopla. If I do think so myself, I am well liked, and respected by most inmates and officers at T.D.C. But the news quickly spread anyway, as the prison grapevine is the best there is. But I was not that excited, I think I knew in my heart already that I was going to make parole this time.

Plus I already had to make decisions about where to go, and what I would be facing when I got out. It was really scary, but I wouldn't let that feeling take hold. Of course I had no idea after nineteen years what exactly I would be facing. I know it was not going too easy at my age, and with having an impairment of my hearing. I have no reliable information to base my decisions with. I have to rely on what other people are telling me, or promised me.

Marilyn a friend; promised me a nice place to live, and help me with all the things I would need, and etc. Larry my late sister's husband, bless his heart was just there, and with all his problems with the DUI's, and his past bad history with law enforcement I wasn't sure I would be allowed to parole out to him. So I was taking it day -by-day, but I have put Marilyn down as my first choice on my list, but have landed up here at Larry's, I don't know how that happened, but here I am going crazy.

As I am thinking, I remember an incident that happened when we were all lined up on a sidewalk waiting for something or another. Barbara, who is an inmate friend of mine, and is in her sixties, leaned over towards me, and whispered into my ear. The officer yelled for her to get back into line. Barbara told me later that he thought she was kissing me. I almost fell out laughing, and by the time I got back to the dorm, people were coming by my house, saying, "Why were you and Barbara kissing out on the sidewalk?" As they were giving me the horse laugh."

CHAPTER NINE

As I am sitting here thinking, well it is September in the year of 2012, wow; I am finally getting out of prison. It is happening so suddenly, one minute I am in my bunk, and the next minute I am packing. An officer come in, and said, "Pack up Martin, I will be back in ten minutes, you are getting out of here." I hurried myself so fast that I kept dropping things, but even then, I was waiting by the door when the officer came back. (It was more like an hour later.) They processed me, and as I left the front gate, my brother-in-law Larry was waiting in a car for me. We drove all the way to Azle, Texas about a six hour drive to where he lived; bless his heart, with all his problems he took me in.

I am out of prison "Yeay", but I am a nervous wreck already. This may be the biggest trial of my life. Everything is so complicated, as I have to depend on someone else for my transportation, no matter where I have to go, or want to go. I am blessed that my niece has taken me down to the Social Security office in Fort Worth to get my social security started. Not much help there as they only want to pay me $680/month, then they (Social Security) take out a $100 or so for Medicare, which leaves me only about $500 to live on. That really knocked me back on my heels. I'm trying to figure out how to live properly on that. But I put God in control, and he has promised to provide, and strengthen me.

My Brother-in-law Larry; who I am paroled out to, is a real sweetheart. I can live here forever if, I close my eyes to the typical old widow mess. He loves animals, and the place is crawling in fleas, cats, and dogs, and they are running all over the place. I already got rid of most of them. If I could keep him from feeding them, they would probably leave on their own, but I don't go there. I went to get my hair cut today, and they would not cut it because I had hair lice in my hair! I believe I handled that quite well; I did not scream or threaten to kill Larry on the spot. But I did have a few tears for a few minutes. I decided it was a first time for everything, and I don't want to miss out on anything in life from now on. I keep telling myself that I want to experience everything life has to offer. But, I'm sure burning my God's ears these days.

Larry is also on probation, the court took his driver's license, so he is not supposed to be driving. But he is my transportation to these meetings, and all of the other places I need to go when my niece is not available. It makes my hair stand on end, and I even started to bite my nails when I'm riding with him. Because if we are stopped by the police for any reason, we could both be back in jail for parole violations. If I don't make the parole meetings, I can be revoked, and go back to jail, so here I am. Larry lives out in the country, outside of Azle, Texas, and it is a small town, and there is no transportation available there, not even a taxi. Most of the parole meetings are in Fort Worth Texas, about twenty miles from Azle. Parole requires you to attend certain meetings that are mandatory, and you have no choice but to be there—no matter what.

As I am thinking back, I keep telling myself why I hate Texas, more than usual anyways. Eudora purchased me a couple of CD's while I was in prison, just before she passed away. They are not all that much as the interest rates have been zilch these past years, but that is all I have in savings. I knew that Social Security would count them off, so I tried to put them in Eddy's name. I had no idea that even with his power of attorney; I could not just transfer them into his name. The bank said no can do, I can't do that, and I would have to cash them in to be put into his name. Cashing them in at that time would cost me $500.00 in penalties, because the CD's would not mature until next year sometime. Of course I wasn't willing to take that loss, so decided to keep them until next year.

It seems that turning them in would be a bad decision on my part also, as when I went to social security they questioned every asset I had. These questions were asked with a risk of penalty of perjury if not answered correctly. About two weeks later I received a letter saying that I had been disqualified for any benefits at all. If I had to live entirely off of the CD's, they would probably last about a year. So now it looks like I will have to bite the bullet, and pull the CD's out anyway, take the loss, appeal the decision at social security, and pray for mercy.

Social Security will of course want to know down to the last penny what I did with them, and for what. Now the bank says, they don't think I can put them in Eddy's name, even if social security would accept that, because he is in prison. But of course I am not accepting any of that because my Father in heaven owns the Bank, Social Security, and all that. So I gave the whole problem over to the Lord, I know that things will work out for my best interest because I love him, and he cares for all my needs, and I know how things will go in my soap opera.

On Monday a few days later, Jo Ann my niece and I went to two different banks trying to get the CD's taken care of. I pulled everything out of the Bank of America, and went to Chase bank in Fort Worth, because Larry banked there. He knows a guy who works there, and he takes care of Larry's finances. I talk with him concerning my situation, and I like the way he talked to me, and also I liked what he proposed, so I turned it all over to him. There is so much information, and decisions to make that my poor brain went numb. I remember in prison, reading about it somewhere not to make too many decisions when you first get out, because of the fact that you haven't made decisions in so long that you are almost incapable of doing so. I believe that, but that's all I've done is make decisions since I got out, and it looks as though I still have quite a few decisions left to make. But the good thing is, that after all the decision making that I have done, my brain seems to be adapting to it, as I am thinking more and more about the problems, and I am making better decisions.

Jo Ann and I left the bank, and she drove us to her place. Now, more decisions for me to make; Jo Ann and her husband own a really nice place about ten acres near Springtown. She says, "Why don't you get a trailer, you can put it here, and set it up to live in."

I said, "You know! That really sounds like a really good solution to some of my problems, if you don't mind me living so close, of course."

"I wouldn't have mentioned it if I didn't mean it, but I hope you do." She said.

"Okay, we can go shopping for a trailer tomorrow, or whenever you can." I said. I spent the night there watching some DVD's. I am still having trouble with these new fan-dangled electronic gadgets, like my cell phone, (Yes I do have one) television remote control, and of course computers. People here are trying to help me by talking me through them, but it isn't working out to well, I guess I will learn after trial and error, or if I had the instruction booklet, or whatever, I might follow that and learn to operate whatever it may be.

Tuesday Jo Ann drove me back to Larry's, and on Thursday Jo Ann came over and drove me to Fort Worth to see my Parole officer. My parole officer told me she is coming for another home visit on the sixteenth of the month, as she has already been there once before, although she never came inside the house. I don't think she is too pleased with me living there, as she asked me about going to a halfway house. More decisions, I was hoping to hang in here until I can get my driver's license. But don't know when that is going to happen, as I can't get one without my birth certificate. It has been weeks since I sent a form to Waurika, Oklahoma where I was born, to have them send it to me, and as yet, I haven't heard from them.

Larry's place is really bad, his niece, and her boyfriend are staying there, they are so lazy, they sit around, and just leave their mess laying there, and I told them that I was not going to clean up after them anymore. Larry just sits around in his underwear, smokes, and sleeps. Then once in a while he goes to some joint in Fort Worth to shoot pool, he says that's about 20 miles each way, and he rides his bicycle, because he is on parole, he is not supposed to do either, ride his bike, (because he is not supposed to go over the county line,) or go to the club, (because of his parole he cannot drink, or take any kind of drugs).

But I am at his mercy to go anywhere, or get anything done. It is very frustrating for me, as I am a person that has to do things, and not just sit around, he did drive me to the library, thank God, now I have something to read. The television is not working, I don't know why, so I still don't know who our new president is, and I keep forgetting to ask anyone; I guess it won't make any difference anyway.

Well my brother-in-law Larry got himself arrested, and he spent the last six weeks in jail, then they let him go with nothing on him, no fines or nothing, they dropped his parole, and gave him back his driver's license. That is good news for him, God must be smiling on him, although I don't think he deserves it. They gave him a big break about two years ago, giving him two years probation instead of some prison time, and he just thumbed his nose at them, by doing as he pleases, driving without a valid driver's license, and going to clubs, etc., crossing the county line, then they put him in jail for a few weeks, then let him go free.

What makes me so angry, which I know is ungodly behavior for me, but I know good people that are innocent or basically so, rotting in prison who can't get out, no matter what they do, I know God has a reason in all he does, but I sure have a hard time with things like that.

I am proud of myself, as I finally got all the lice out of my hair and got my hair cut, although it cost me forty dollars. Larry called a friend he knew that worked in a hair salon, and made me an appointment. Larry drove me to my last parole meeting, and after that, he drove me to the salon; It is in an expensive area of town. I was surprised that Larry even knew someone working at a place like that."

Well it is now December 2012, and I just received my birth certificate, and my niece is coming to take me to Fort Worth to take my driver's license test. On the way, I say to Jo Ann, "Don't you think that I should see if I can still drive?"

Jo Ann says, "Yes I do you can drive in there," and swings the car into some church's parking area.

"Oh thank you so much and bless you," I say to her, as I get behind the wheel.

I drive around the church area a few times, and it felt good. I guess it's like once you learn to ride a bike, you never forget how, the only thing with that saying is, I never learned to ride a bike. I studied the driver's handbook, and had to take the written test on a computer, (of which I know nothing about, and really don't want to). I managed to complete the test, (with the help from a very nice person working there) and I passed with an 80 score. The test requires you to Parallel Park, so Jo Ann let me practice a couple of times between people testing. I passed that too, and yea, I got my driver's license. That is a biggie, the next biggie is getting a car.

Then Jo Ann and I went shopping for a trailer, and all the trailers in trailer lot's are to expensive, so I got a newspaper, and looked for used trailers. After looking for a couple of hours, I purchased a trailer we had looked at earlier, and the guy that sold it to me pulled it out to Jo Ann's place, and set it up for me. Jo Ann let me drive her car, so he followed us. Seeing how I was at their place, and it was getting late, and it was getting around dinner time, Jo Ann and Chuck talked me into staying the night.

The next morning Jo Ann dropped me off at Larry's place, he had been outside doing something for quite a while, and no sooner than he came in he says, "Look Eva can you give me some money so I can go buy some tobacco."

"Larry," I said, "I will give you money for a lot of things, but buying that whack y tobacco, and or drugs with it," (although he doesn't have to worry about that anymore) but I have to refuse." I didn't think it was marijuana, because it didn't smell like it, but I don't think it was normal tobacco.

"Okay, if you won't give me money for that," Larry says, "Then I have no choice, I want you to leave here, and you will have to find another place to live."

"Okay, if that's the way you want it, I will leave right away." I say to him.

As I am staring at him, I get out my cell phone, and call Jo Ann, as she answers her phone, she says, "Hello! Jo Ann here."

"Hello Jo Ann, this is Eva, and I know you just left here a little while ago, and I want to thank you for that, and I wanted to tell you that Larry just kicked me out. Would you mind coming back here, and get me?"

"Eva, just hang in there," Jo Ann says, "I am on my way, don't even worry about it, I will be there within a half hour."

"Oh thank you," I say, "and bless you, I will be ready when you get here."

I go into where I have been sleeping, and pick up all my stuff, and pack my bag, and I am waiting at the door when Larry come over to me and says, "Maybe I was to hasty Eva, you don't have to leave."

I answer back, "It is okay, I was going to leave anyway, as I bought a trailer to live in, and it is at Jo Ann's place, and I am going to live in it. I had planned to tell you later, and I want to thank you for everything you have done for me."

Eva gives him a hug, and he says to her, "I am sorry it turned out this way, but maybe it is for the best," as he gives her a hug, and a kiss on the cheek.

Jo Ann arrives a few minutes later, and I say to her, "Thank you so much for coming back, as I know you were just here a little while ago, and I really do appreciate everything that you have, and or will do for me."

Jo Ann says, "Eva don't worry about it, I enjoy doing things for you, I want to be of any help that I can."

I put my stuff into her car, and away we go, and Jo Ann says, "What happened there?"

"Larry asked me for some money," I answered, "So he could buy some whacky tobacco, and I told him no."

"So after all he has done for you, are you still mad at him for kicking you out?" Jo Ann says.

"No I am not mad, we made up, and I apologized to him, and I gave him some money for the rent."

I had to sleep inside their house because the weather turned so nasty, and we had to wait until the storm was over to start work on cleaning up the trailer. The used trailer needs a lot of work, and Chuck bless his heart, offered to do most of the work, so I can move into it.

Jo Ann and Chuck have been so nice to drive me everywhere looking for a car for me, using their time, and gas. Of course they are both retired, but still most people wouldn't be bothered. I just hope someday I will be able to repay them for all their kindness.

Well I finally found a car, a 2001 Chevrolet, I really do like it, it runs, and drives real good. I took it to a mechanic anyway, and he looked it over. The Mechanic said, "It is good to go, at least for now."

The insurance is a big problem too, seeing that I have not had any driving records for the past nineteen years, and the fees are pretty high, but hopefully it will drop in time. It really feels good not to have to depend on any one to take me anywhere. I can go where, and when I want, and where I have to go without bothering Jo Ann, who has been so good to me, and she hasn't complained at all.

Well now that I got all of that all taken care of, I am going to get some dentures, and a better hearing aid, then I will be able to function better. I went to two different dentists, and each one wanted about $4000, to pull the rest of my teeth, and put in new dentures, and that does not include any follow up appointments. Now I'm going nuts, trying to decide which dentist to go to, and if I really want to let go of all that much money.

Also I went to have my ears checked, and that was another hit in the pocket book. They want $1,400 for each ear, and I need two. God is so good, I put all my trust into him, and he has taken care of me. I am so grateful for everyone who has helped me out, even Larry who kicked me out. I finally heard from social security, and God is really good! The notice said I would be getting $900.00 a month instead of $600.00/month so that is a miracle in itself, I am so grateful for all this, and I can't stop thanking my Lord.

Now I am working on how to make my cell phone work, I can't even think about the computer. Besides my seven year old great, great niece gives me a terrible inferiority complex by playing chess on the computer, and beating it. I can't even play chess at all, much less on the computer. She is an amazing little girl, mostly because Jo Ann and

Chuck take the time to teach her everything she wants to know, and she wants to know it all. She's had one spanking in all her little life, and that was because she was crawling through the dogie door, and into the back yard, where the swimming pool is. She was around a year old at the time, I think god had a hand in someone finding her before she got to the pool.

THE END

www.ingramcontent.com/pod-product-compliance
Lightning Source LLC
LaVergne TN
LVHW040157080526
838202LV00042B/3208